TRUE CRIME HAS NEVER
BEEN MORE READABLE . . .
OR DISTURBING.

To Love, Honor . . . and Kill explores the psychology
of murderers who kill those closest to them. Cool,
deliberate slayings and acts committed in a fit of
passion are hauntingly examined. Here are mysterious and bizarre cases of both love and hate.

**"There are only about twenty murders a year in
London, and not all are serious; some are just husbands killing their wives."**

—A Police Commander in London, England

TO LOVE, HONOR . . .
AND KILL

TO LOVE, HONOR... AND Kill

Clifford L. Linedecker

KNIGHTSBRIDGE PUBLISHING COMPANY
NEW YORK

Published in the United States by
Knightsbridge Publishing Company
255 East 49th Street
New York, New York 10017

ISBN: 1-877961-26-4

10 9 8 7 6 5 4 3 2 1
FIRST EDITION

*To the victims, and to those
who love and miss them.*

ACKNOWLEDGMENTS

Books dealing with true events do not come into being solely through the efforts of the authors, but are the result of the cooperation of many people. Some of the people and organizations the author wishes to thank for their kind and expeditious assistance in the compilation of this book include:

Richard E. Harney, publisher of the *Parke County Sentinel* in Rockville, Indiana; Patty Bryant of the *Tribune-Star* Publishing Co. in Terre Haute, Indiana; journalists Martin Turner and Gerry Brown, of London, England; B.M. Murray of the *Union-Tribune* library in San Diego, California; Rusty Cunningham, managing editor/news, and Denise I. Hintermeister, librarian, at the *Quad-City Times* in

Davenport, Iowa; F. Kirk Powell, editor and publisher of the *Holden Progress* in Holden, Kansas; Don Morton, librarian, Sedalia Public Library, Kansas; Tom Thompson, and Thomas Christman, news editor of *The Peninsula Daily News* in Port Angeles, Washington; Betty Scott, of the *Miami-Herald* library in Fort Lauderdale, Florida; Mr. Bell at the Greensboro News and Record library in Greensboro, North Carolina; and photograher Eddie Motes of the *Anniston Star*, Anniston, Alabama.

Thanks are also due to the many others who took the time to talk with me about individual cases and share their knowledge of complex points of criminology and legal strategems.

Special notes of appreciation are due to my agent, Dawson Taylor, and to my editor, Colleen Dimson.

The accounts of conjugal murders presented here are as true and factual as it has been possible to make them, based on the documents and other information available to me, and the recall of witnesses or participants. No names, places or events have been changed.

TABLE OF CONTENTS

INTRODUCTION

We feel almost the same revulsion toward conjugal slayings — the murder of one life partner by another — as we do about the murder of a child. When a husband or wife is killed by their spouse, it is the worst possible betrayal, because the murderer is the individual the man or woman should be able to most trust. Yet, it is a shockingly common form of homicide.

It is so common, in fact, that when a married man or woman becomes a homicide victim, almost invariably the first person that police turn to as a potential suspect is the spouse. Studies have shown that almost seventy percent of the murders in North America are committed by someone known to the victim: a friend, acquaintance — or a family member.

All too common incidents of wife abuse account for many such slayings. Almost daily, somewhere in North America, a wife is beaten to death, strangled or shot by an abusive husband. Usually the beatings and assaults, which have sometimes begun during courtship, continue for months or years before the fatal attack.

Brutal husbands also die at the hands of wives who, after long-standing provocation, finally react by committing the ultimate violent act.

But there are other conjugal murders that are less predictable. Unlike those slayings that result from the mindless violence of spouse abuse, they are carefully plotted in advance, sometimes with lovers or hirelings.

Cool, deliberate slayings. They are invariably crimes of greed and passion, because money and sex can provide powerful motivation for the murder of a spouse after love has cooled.

The desire to profit financially from the death of a spouse figures in a majority of the ten true crime stories presented here. Other murders occurred because a spouse had found someone else they preferred as a playmate and lover. However, some stories defy any easy categorizing.

An effort has been made to select recent slayings that are mysterious or bizarre, and to take them from a broad geographical area. Attention has also been given to providing a mix of economic and social classes because conjugal murders, like spouse and child abuse, are not restricted to either the poor or the rich.

No attempt has been made to arrive at any earthshaking conclusions about the root causes of conjugal slayings or how they can be stopped. Serious researchers in the fields of criminology and corrections, sociology, psychology and psychiatry have been looking for viable answers far longer than I. And it seems they are no closer than I am to sorting out either the reasons or possible solutions.

It is impossible, however, to undertake a project such as this without arriving at a few conclusions. The cases examined here, and others I've investigated but which are not included in the collection, seem to illustrate that there is a definite difference between men and women in their approach to carrying out the murder of an unwanted spouse.

The belief that women kill by poisoning or other quiet methods appears to have some legitimacy. Based on murders I've become familiar with during some twenty years as a police and criminal court reporter, and another ten years as an editor and freelance crime writer, and excepting only the random violence of the slums, I've found the female of the species much more likely than the male to resort to a "hands-off" method of dispatching her mate.

She is more likely to use poison, or to pay someone else — either with sex, money, or other material goods — to do the dirty work for her. When she is forced to do the killing herself, she uses a gun. This type of weapon still distances a killer somewhat from her grisly handiwork. The act of pulling a trigger so that a bullet slams into a body some inches or feet away, does not require the gut-churning close contact called for when plunging a knife into living flesh, or strangling, drowning or beating someone to death.

Guns seem to be equally common as weapons for both male and female killers. But the hands-on forms of killing are employed almost exclusively by the stronger, more aggressive male. And males seldom use poison.

Finally, the reader is almost certainly to be struck, as I was, by the disparity and hypocrisy in the sentencing of convicted killers.

Today's life sentences do not mean that the convicted criminal will spend the rest of his or her life behind bars. The life sentence ordered for one of the killers examined in this book was handed down with the stipulation that there would be no possibility of parole for seven or ten years. Actually, ten years is the average time served by persons convicted of murder today.

In the rare cases where the death penalty is ordered for someone who has cold-bloodedly plotted and carried out a murder, appeals can drag on for years. No matter how innocent their victim or how depraved and cruel the manner of murder selected, few conjugal killers are executed today — not even those sentenced to death. Despite public demands for a stronger hand in dealing with violent crime, legislatures and the courts continue to equivocate, and fail to make the punishment fit the crime.

Instead, killers, rapists and other dangerous criminals are more likely to be held for a time in prisons where, at taxpayers' expense, they may take up oil painting, weight lifting, the study of law, or earn college degrees until they are paroled or their death sentences are commuted and they are released.

There are no oil paintings, no college courses — and no appeals for their victims.

CHAPTER ONE

DEATH IN A HOG LOT

There's little to distinguish tiny Cayuga, Indiana, from hundreds of other sleepy farming communities throughout the Midwest except its history as a onetime rail center from which hogs were shipped to nearby Terre Haute, then loaded on barges for a trip down the Wabash River on to the Mississippi and finally to New Orleans.

Today's farm animals headed for slaughter are more likely to be transported by trucks, but pork production is still an important business for area farmers and hog lots are spotted throughout the rolling west-central Indiana countryside.

Hog lots are for hogs, however — not for the bodies of men, like the wind-chilled corpse found facedown on the frozen mud of a lot near Lodi, a few miles due east of Cayuga.

If Cayuga is a small town, with just over a thousand residents, Lodi is a mere flyspeck. With a population of a dozen or so, it's so small it doesn't even appear on some road maps.

It was a crisply cold Saturday morning, February 25, 1984, when an area resident returning from a trip to Cayuga spotted a body while driving past a farm at about seven-thirty. Afraid the body might be that of his son who farmed the property, he drove on to his son's home, and after determining the victim was someone else, returned to the lot with his daughter-in-law. He stayed in the lot to keep the pigs away from the body while she telephoned the Parke County Sheriff's Department.

When Chief Deputy Mark Bridge arrived a short time later he found that the victim's pockets had been turned inside out. Several objects including a flashlight, cigarette lighter, billfold — and an identification card from the General Motors Corporation plant in Danville, Illinois, were scattered near the body.

The card, which was lying outside the billfold a few feet from the corpse, carried the name of Marion L. Stonebraker, Sr.

The officer immediately recognized the name as that of a man reported missing by his family in a call to the sheriff's department several hours earlier. Stonebraker, who lived near Cayuga with his wife, Loretta, was a lifetime resident of the area and a member of the large and well-known Stonebraker clan.

Stonebraker was fifty-one years old with thinning red hair that had earned him the predictably unimaginative nickname "Red." That red hair had now been bloodied by a gaping bullet wound that had ripped through the back of his skull.

There was no gun visible at the scene, and suspecting that the victim might have pitched forward on top of the weapon, Deputy Bridge rolled the body over. He didn't find a gun, but there was another bullet wound in the victim's nose. It was not possible to determine if this injury was caused by a second bullet or if it was an entry or exit wound from the same round that had damaged the back of the victim's head. Bridge rolled the body back to its original position.

The vanguard of a rapidly growing contingent of law officers and civilians who had heard about the body had begun to arrive. Parke County Sheriff Mike Eslinger, Detective John Britton, state police and sheriff's deputies from nearby counties crowded into the hog lot. One of Red's brothers, Miles Sherman Stonebraker, Red's son, Marion Stonebraker, Jr., and a friend who had all been searching for him since his wife Loretta had reported him missing, were among the first of his family to show up. They identified the victim and when his son stooped down and checked his father's pockets, he advised the deputy that a coin purse was missing.

After the body was removed to the Vermillion County Hospital at Clinton for an autopsy,

Sheriff Eslinger was quoted in early news accounts as saying the case was being treated as a suicide, even though no weapon had been recovered. He pointed out that animals, especially hogs, had been known to pick up objects in their mouths and carry them around, and Stonebraker's body had been found next to a round barn in a three-acre lot which enclosed both hogs and cattle. Even though some twenty law enforcement officers had spread out and spent several hours in a Sunday search of the lot without success, it was, nevertheless, still considered a possibility that the death weapon could have been overlooked.

Sheriff Eslinger made it plain, however, that the investigation was not locked into suicide as a probable cause of Stonebraker's mysterious death. "We are a long way from being done with the investigation," he cautioned.

The prophetic nature of the sheriff's words became apparent after the autopsy report was disclosed. Headed by Parke County Coroner Dr. Peggy Sankey, pathologists turned up a lead fragment, but no bullet, inside Stonebraker's head.

More significantly, Dr. Sankey, who had performed more than a thousand autopsies during her career, determined that Stonebraker was shot in the center of the back of the head, and the small caliber slug had coursed upward, ricocheting off the skull through the brain. After examining Dr. Sankey's report, x-rays and a damaged portion of the victim's skull, another expert from the Indiana School of

Medicine concluded that, although the bullet had been fired at close range, the gun was not held flush against the head, as is common in gunshot suicides.

Inspection of Stonebraker's nose injury also failed to turn up any powder residue, which would have been present if it had been a close-range entry wound.

The autopsy made it clear that it would have been physically impossible for Stonebraker to have held a rifle or handgun to the back of his head at the angle indicated by the entry wound and by the trajectory of the slug as it smashed through his skull. The shooting had to have been carried out by someone else, and Parke County law enforcement authorities now knew they had a homicide on their hands.

Meanwhile, the victim's large family had gathered at the DeVerter Brothers Funeral Home in Cayuga to say their final farewells. In addition to his son and widow, Stonebraker left behind seven stepchildren, four grandchildren, sixteen great-grandchildren, a sister, and four brothers, one of whom had also been married to the dead man's wife, Loretta.

Friends later recalled that the widow seemed understandably shaken at her loss. But she didn't complain when Red's son, Marion, Jr., reached into the casket and took a winged skull necklace from around his father's neck. He also dropped a letter, written when he was eleven years old, into the casket.

As the family mixed and exchanged condolences and words of grief, there was also hushed conversation about the deceased's insurance and how it might be distributed. Red had been a firm believer in insurance, so much so that he sometimes complained that he was "insurance poor." Some family members estimated that Red had carried at least $60,000 in insurance, maybe as much as $100,000.

Not all the sympathy was reserved for the widow. There was also concern for Marion, Jr., or "Bud" or "Buddy," as he was more commonly known to his family and friends. His life hadn't been a bed of roses even before his father's sudden death.

Bud, who was in his mid-twenties, had been living on welfare and hadn't worked since February, 1981. When asked to help search for his father, he was so broke he had to borrow three dollars to buy gas. Later he drove to Terre Haute and borrowed more money so he could attend his father's funeral.

There was no question that Bud had known hard times, but they were no worse, it seemed, than some of the hard-luck cards fate had dealt to his stepmother, Loretta. Like most of her family, friends and neighbors, she knew first-hand what it was like to be poor.

Loretta had been barely ten years old when her family showed up in the Cayuga area and set up housekeeping in a tent. Most winters in central Indiana are snowy and bitter cold; the summers are blistering hot; and the springtime is wet and muddy. Living in a tent was miserable, and after about two years, the head of the family built a three-room house for the large brood. The modest home had a living room, kitchen and bedroom; and the toilet was an outhouse.

Loretta was twelve when an older male relative sexually molested her. In order to protect Loretta, her mother sent her to Oklahoma to live with other family members. But two or three years later, after dropping out of school in the eighth grade, Loretta was back and married to Miles Stonebraker. Babies came in a hurry, and before she was nineteen she had four children. The kids and the housekeeping kept her working from dawn to dusk, and after ten years she called it quits, and she and Miles were divorced.

Life didn't get any easier for her as a divorcée in her mid-twenties with four kids. Many nights the little family had nothing to eat but thin water-gravy, soup beans or macaroni. In the late summer, if they were lucky, there were wild blackberries to pick and eat. Yet, even during those hardscrabble times, Loretta developed a reputation for taking in strays and sharing her meager food and shelter with others who were even more needy.

Then, in 1981, fifteen years after her divorce and after a whirlwind courtship of barely two months she married her former brother-in-law, Red Stonebraker. Loretta admitted to intimates that she didn't love him, but he was a good provider and she was sick and tired of poverty. Red was a hard worker and had a good job as a core maker in the General Motors foundry just across the state line from Vermil-

lion County, in Danville, Illinois. By 1984, he
was pulling in a solid $28,000 a year, and he
wasn't stingy!

When children and stepchildren, alone or
with friends, wives and babies, stopped by at
the house to share meals with Red and Loretta
they were made welcome. A frequent visitor,
Buddy often sampled their hospitality and
when some of Loretta's children needed help,
Red readily agreed to sign notes so they could
buy house trailers. The young couples parked
the trailers near the family homestead in
Cayuga.

It wasn't long before a little settlement had
grown-up around the house which was across
the street from a brickyard and in a run-down
area known locally as Pumpkin Center.

Married twice before, Red's first marriage
to Buddy's mother ended in divorce, and his
second wife died. Although he had developed
a reputation through the years as an enthusi-
astic outdoorsman who liked doing nothing
better than hunting or fishing with his cro-
nies, he sold all of his fishing gear and almost
entirely gave up those pursuits so he could
spend more time with Loretta and the family.

A devoted family man once again, Red
stuffed his billfold with photographs of stepchildren, their spouses and youngsters. He
turned over the family finances to Loretta,
easily agreeing to accept a fifty-dollar per
week allowance out of his paycheck to offset
the costs of gasoline for his pickup truck,
tobacco, and other personal needs. Despite his

generosity, Loretta wasn't satisfied. Almost ten years older than she was, Red worked long hours at an exhausting job, and didn't much feel like kicking-up his heels and partying when he got home. She still wanted to enjoy some of the good times she may have felt she was cheated out of when she was younger, and she kept the house jumping with people. When she wasn't surrounded by family and friends at home, she was apt to be out dancing or sipping a few cool ones with friends at local watering holes.

A few stories made the rounds about trouble between Loretta and her husband, but in general he seemed to be tolerant of his wife's search for good times, even though his innate jealous streak occasionally surfaced.

Red especially resented his wife's close friendship with Big Helen and the time they spent together.

Helen Williams was a huge, slow-witted woman, who was not so much fat as just plain big. At a hulking six-feet and solid 265 pounds, she loomed over almost all the women she knew and most of the men. She had a surprisingly soft baby face framed with short cropped hair, but she was tough and liked to prove that she could be as strong and mean as any man. She was also a lesbian.

Big Helen, or "Big H" as she was also sometimes called, was born in Eugene, a settlement of some three hundred people almost within hollering distance of Cayuga's northwest town limits. She made it to the ninth grade before she dropped out of Kingman School because she couldn't read or write well enough to keep up with the classwork. By the time she was eighteen, she got her first job with the carnivals, working game booths at county fairs and eventually driving semi-tractor-trailer trucks for the shows when they were on the road.

During off-seasons for the shows, she found other work unloading trucks at a lumber yard, and filling in catch-can at whatever manual labor happened to be available. When times were especially hard, she moved in with her parents, camped in a trailer behind their home, slept in her car or bunked with friends.

Big Helen had been married to two men, the first time for only one month. The second marriage lasted five years, but Helen later admitted that her relationships with men were merely a cover-up to hide her homosexuality.

In 1981, she participated in an unorthodox double wedding. Invitations were mailed announcing Big Helen's marriage to another woman, as well as the marriage of two other lesbians. The couples shared a three-tiered wedding cake, and Helen was dressed in a blue tuxedo with a ruffled shirt, while her bride wore a traditional white bridal gown for the ceremony. Big Helen's fellow groom was a muscular woman who drove long-haul tractor-trailer trucks and identified herself on CB radio as the "Moonlight Bandit."

At one time Big Helen and Loretta stayed together near Catlin, Illinois, for nearly two years, swapping their labor for room and board with a farmer Loretta had dated. They had met through Loretta's children, who made friends with Big Helen during one of the area fairs.

Although Loretta had known her for years, she'd lost track of her friend until one day she saw a poster advertising a mud-wrestling event at the county fair, and featuring Big Helen as one of the gladiators.

When Loretta looked up her old friend, Big Helen had already landed a full-time job with the town of Cayuga as a ditchdigger for the water department, and there wasn't a man on the crew who could keep up with her. But because she liked the carny life, she was moonlighting as a mud wrestler. She sometimes wrestled John C. Sigler, a husky young cousin of Loretta's, at local fairs and benefits, and she once outgrappled a local male television personality from Terre Haute.

She enjoyed besting males in contests of strength and physical skill. And she was respected for her expertise and courage as a driver in demolition derbies, where she earned trophies in competition against some of the best. But her competitive nature against males could also turn mean, and ugly stories circulated about the men and boys she had beaten up or humiliated.

Once she punched a man in the face, leaving him badly bloodied, and another time she was part of a gang that beat up a young man at one of the carnivals. During the melee, his shoes were burnt, and he was smashed face down on the ground and told to "screw the dirt." Big Helen denied her responsibility for the last two actions when she was questioned about the brawl. Nevertheless, she was fired from the shows after the one-sided fracas. Regardless of how large a part she had played in the incident, the message was clear: although her personality was generally placid, there were times when she could be as mean as a peach orchard boar.

About the time Loretta renewed her friendship with the big bruising mud wrestler, Big Helen was having trouble supporting herself, and broke up with the "wife" she had married in the bizarre double wedding. She sold her television set, and gradually got rid of most of her personal property because of her need for money.

After a while she moved in with the Stonebrakers, where she cleaned house and also helped with any outdoor chores calling for muscle and strength. She was always willing to lend a hand when there was a hard job to do.

And Loretta had a very hard job for her — she wanted her husband killed. As Red was heavily insured, Loretta said, she would pay her friend $1,500 to get rid of him.

Big Helen wasn't against a little violence if the timing and the reasons seemed right. She had beaten men up when they angered her, and one night after downing about twenty shots of whiskey she had even smashed the windshields of several cars parked in the driveway of a relative's service station — but murder was something else. She didn't want to do it, so Loretta upped the price to $2,500 and promised Big Helen that she could permanently make her home with her.

At Loretta's suggestion, Big Helen got in touch with one of her former wrestling opponents, twenty-year-old John Sigler, the sturdy 265-pound youth who was a first cousin of Loretta. Big Helen brought Sigler, who had been a special education student at the Turkey Run School Corporation, to the Stonebraker home where they discussed the murder scheme. But Big Helen and Sigler were still not convinced they should kill a man, even for $2,500.

A few days later Big Helen, Sigler and another man drove to Florida to look for jobs in an old car which Big Helen had bought for one hundred dollars. The Stonebrakers threw a going-away party for them the night before they left — and Loretta raised her offer to $3,000. She also fried some chicken for her friends to eat on the trip.

By the time Big Helen and Sigler got to Florida they had experienced so much car trouble they were out of money. So they dropped their companion off at a friend's house, and less than an hour later were on their way back to Cayuga, flat broke. On the way back Big Helen and Sigler agreed that they would do the job. Sigler would be the hit man, and use an old .22 bolt-action Hamilton rifle he was carrying with him in a suitcase.

After talking the project over with Loretta, it was decided that they would lure their victim to a hog lot by talking him into helping them steal a pig for butchering. The lot would not only offer a secluded location for the slaying, they reasoned, but Loretta had also assured them that the hogs would destroy the evidence by eating the body.

On Friday afternoon, February 24, Red returned home and handed his paycheck to Loretta, who cashed it at a Cayuga bank, then gave him his fifty-dollar allowance, and another five dollars to gas up the truck. Then Loretta and Big Helen walked onto the back porch where Loretta handed her friend two ice picks. She told Big Helen to stab Red at the base of his neck, but Big Helen refused to consider using an ice pick for the slaying as Sigler already had a gun for the job.

When Sigler showed up, he and Big Helen drove away to meet Red, who had kissed his wife goodbye and left to buy gas. Loretta stayed home and began cooking up spareribs for her fellow conspirators, whom she expected to be hungry when they returned.

Red parked his truck near a strip coal mine, and transferred to Sigler's car for the approximate two-mile ride to the hog lot. Big Helen watched the two men walk through the dusk toward the round barn, then drove to a nearby store to kill about fifteen minutes before returning to pick up Sigler.

Red was bending over a hog when his companion lifted the .22 rifle he was carrying and shot him in the back of the head. Then Sigler rifled the victim's pockets and took his coin purse, which contained fifty dollars. Red's knife, which was to be used to gut the hog, was left strapped to his leg, still in its sheath.

Back inside his car, Sigler tossed the coin purse on the seat. Big Helen took out the fifty dollars, and when they stopped the vehicle on a bridge over the Wabash River, she threw the empty purse into the water. When they parted, Sigler went to a house party. Big Helen returned to the Stonebraker house and gave the fifty dollars to Loretta. Loretta pulled a twenty-dollar bill from her purse for beer, and gave it to Big Helen. After Big Helen returned with the drinks, the two women and several other house guests, who were unaware of the slaying, ate the spareribs Loretta had prepared while her husband was being killed.

But Loretta had made a major mistake! As experienced hog farmers know, only brood sows with baby pigs will eat people. Feeder hogs usually will not, and the lot near Lodi was home to feeder hogs and cattle, not to brood sows.

Assuming the role of a concerned spouse the evening of the murder, Loretta began telephoning family and friends, area hospitals and police with reports that her husband was missing. The authorities were told he had been despondent lately and was known to have been spending much of his time at a cemetery, grieving at his mother's grave.

Loretta, who had suffered a small accident, was at St. Elizabeth's Hospital in Danville when Red's body was found and identified. When a friend had asked to borrow a punch bowl for a wedding, Big Helen had accidentally cracked or bruised Loretta's ribs as she boosted her up so she could reach into a cabinet for the dish.

The women were waiting in the hospital emergency room when one of Loretta's daughters telephoned and told Big Helen: "Bring Mom home, but don't say nothing to her. We found Red."

Red was more heavily insured than most of his relatives had ever guessed. He had taken out eleven policies with five companies for a total of $162,250, and Loretta was the sole beneficiary.

She doled out her murder-for-hire payments to Big Helen and Sigler a bit at a time as she received checks from the various policies. At one time she counted out $1,700 to Big Helen in crisp fifty-dollar bills, warning her both to keep her mouth shut and refrain from spending the money around Cayuga. And she advised the huge mud wrestler to also caution Sigler in the same way. Loretta was worried. Someone had been telephoning death threats to the house, and even with Big Helen to protect her, she was frightened.

Loretta was generous with her family after Red's death and passed out money to help pay bills and get them through the hard times that many of them seemed chronically unable to shake. She also paid the bills for oral surgery and false teeth for one of Big Helen's occasional lovers because she thought it would make the woman feel better about herself and help her obtain a job. But with Red gone and insurance money coming in, Loretta also had the time and money to enjoy herself. Dressed up in jeans and a frilly blouse, or a miniskirt and boots, she made the rounds of local taverns with Big Helen to dance or merely sit and tilt a few drinks while holding hands. She and Big Helen danced well together.

A few times, however, friends overheard Big Helen ending an argument with Loretta with the ominous reminder: "Remember the favor I done you!" Visibly shaken, Loretta would reply, "You're talking too much."

Loretta was nevertheless the dominant member of the pair, and generally Big Helen did her best to please her. Once after a disagreement she even submitted to grounding when Loretta restricted her to the property like an unruly teenager. And Loretta laid down the law about Big Helen's carny friends. She didn't want them hanging around, and although Big Helen was disappointed, she meekly complied.

However, the burly mud wrestler wasn't having an easy time dealing with the part she had played in Red's murder. Her stomach began acting up, and she stepped up her drinking just as she had after breaking up with her "wife." She had lost her job digging ditches after a new town council took office, and had a lot of time on her hands. She was drinking a case of beer a day and was drunk much of the time. There was also talk of Big Helen using LSD, speed and marijuana, although she insisted she didn't smoke pot because it made her face swell.

Rapidly tiring of her company, Loretta complained to a woman friend that Big Helen had been invited to stay only for a brief time but had moved in permanently. Finally, Loretta asked Big Helen to move out of the house. There had been too much talk about them and rumors were circulating that Big Helen had something to do with Red's slaying, the widow explained. It would look better if she got out of town for awhile.

Big Helen was devastated. Hopelessly in love with Loretta, she had believed that once Red was disposed of, she and his widow would live together in the house as a permanent twosome. But, obedient as always, she left. She bought a camper attachment designed to fit on pickup trucks, and on the Fourth of July joined the carnival again.

Sigler was also spending his new-found wealth — and carelessly disregarding Loretta's warnings to keep his mouth shut. He liked to drink, smoke pot and party, and sometimes when he drank or was upset, he talked too much.

A friend who shared a house with Sigler's girlfriend and her brother was with him when he produced a handful of fifty-dollar bills, which he said had been given to him by Big Helen. Sigler used some of the bills to buy marijuana and to pay off a bill his friend owed for pot. And once when the two men were at Bird Dog's Tavern in Cayuga, Sigler told him, "I know you know I shot him." Then Sigler warned his friend that he had better not tell anyone what he knew.

Sigler continued to talk too much, telling both his girlfriend and her brother that he had murdered Red. And one time after a nasty quarrel with his girl, he stalked to his pickup truck, got the rifle and held it to his head, threatening to commit suicide.

Also brooding — and talking — Big Helen confessed to her friend the Moonlight Bandit that she had participated in the murder-for-hire plot. Meanwhile, investigators had logged more than fifty telephone calls with tips about the murder. They were especially interested in anonymous telephone calls from a woman who said she knew a lot about the Stonebraker slaying, and named names.

The net was closing on the conspirators.

Sigler was sleeping at his parent's farm home, where he lived and worked, when a policeman knocked at the door and asked the young man to accompany him to the Cayuga Firehouse, which had been set up as a command post for the various law enforcement agencies investigating the Stonebraker murder. The officer told Sigler to bring along any guns he owned.

The youth took a rifle owned by his mother from a gun rack in the bedroom, and climbed into the police car for the drive to the firehouse. Inspection of the rifle quickly determined that it was not the weapon used in the slaying. Sigler denied that he had any other guns, neglecting to mention the murder weapon which he had kept under his girlfriend's bed before taking it to a shop to have it repaired. Except for one time when he had spent a weekend in jail after stealing some gasoline and a battery when he was a teenager, and a few minor brushes with the law over marijuana, Sigler hadn't had much experience with police, and he was nervous. But after the questioning was concluded, he was permitted to return home.

A short time later, however, State Police Investigator Dan Clevenger showed up at his house and specifically asked for the .22 Hamilton. Sigler turned it over to police. The weapon was in terrible shape. The stock had been sawed off to form a pistol grip, the extractor had been removed, there was no firing pin and the bolt had been beaten on with a hammer.

Big Helen was also called to the Cayuga Firehouse for questioning. And in August, a police officer talked with her about Red's slaying and suggested that Sigler had been shooting his mouth off. She was scared to death.

She started to worry about being caught and sentenced to death in the electric chair. Afraid of electricity ever since she was a child, she had seen two people accidentally electrocuted while she was working carnivals and fairs. One of the victims was a teenage boy; the other a man whom she remembered as "lighting up like a Christmas tree." Since then, Big Helen had been careful never to work around dangerous electrical wiring or equipment.

Finally, Big Helen realized that it was only a matter of a few days, or hours, before she would be arrested. She told the Moonlight Bandit,

"I'm just waiting for them to come and get me...I'll be glad when it's over."

She also talked to Cayuga Town Marshal Jerry Weir and asked that he personally make the arrest when the time came, pleading with him not to handcuff her in front of her mother.

About a week later, on September 8, Marshal Weir knocked on the door at the home of Big Helen's parents and placed her under arrest for her part in Red's murder. He didn't handcuff her until she was inside his police car. Loretta was arrested at a Cayuga pool hall, and Sigler was picked up at his parents' home in Kingman. Authorities announced that a huge amount of insurance carried on the life of the foundry worker was the motive for his brutal murder.

Loretta and Sigler both insisted they were innocent, but Big Helen quickly broke down and dictated a written confession to her friend, the Moonlight Bandit, who visited her in jail and urged her to tell the true story.

In February, 1985, on the anniversary of Red's death, a paid notice was published in Clinton's *Daily Clintonian*. Signed by Marion, Jr., (Buddy), and listing other family members, it read:

In Memorium
May the guilty suffer as he must have
before being thrown to the hogs.

Loretta was the first to be tried. Parke County

Prosecutor James O. Hanner accused her of masterminding the slaying in order to collect more than $160,000 in insurance, and she was charged with conspiracy to commit murder and aiding and inducing a murder.

The courtroom was packed with spectators, especially when the star witness, Big Helen, wearing an open-neck, plaid shirt and blue jeans, took the stand. She talked frankly about her romantic relationship with Loretta, with another member of the Stonebraker family, and with other women, revealing glimpses of a tawdry world that was as foreign to most of the jury and spectators as a midnight boatride on the River Volga.

And she detailed the murder plot, explaining how it had been orchestrated by Loretta, and how it was because of her love for Loretta that she had been pulled into the scheme.

The Moonlight Bandit stalked to the witness stand in blue jeans and black boots, and disclosed that she was the woman who had telephoned the anonymous tips to police naming the conspirators in Red's slaying. The witness, who had given up long-haul trucking and was a guard at the federal penitentiary in Terre Haute, said Big Helen told her three times about offers from Loretta to pay big money for Red's murder.

She said she was riding around with Big Helen early in March 1984 when her friend said, "Well, we did it. It's over," and then related how the murder plot was carried out.

Testifying in her own defense, Loretta insisted that she loved her husband and did not plot his death. She also denied that she was homosexual or had a lesbian relationship with Big Helen.

Although her mother had collected more than $100,000 of the insurance, one of Loretta's daughters testified that there was only about $17 left. The witness said her mother had spent only about $3,000 on herself, and "the rest on us kids."

The jury of seven women and five men deliberated two hours before returning a verdict of guilty on both counts. On March 26, 1985, just one week after her forty-fourth birthday and three weeks after the jury finding, Parke Circuit Court Judge Earl Dowd sentenced Loretta to fifty years in prison on the conspiracy charge, and sixty years for aiding and inducing the murder. He ruled that the sentences were to be served concurrently. She would be eligible for parole in approximately thirty years.

"Any less sentence would depreciate the very seriousness of the crime," the judge declared.

As Loretta was sentenced, her husky cousin was being tried in the same Parke County Circuit Court in Rockville on charges of murder and of conspiracy to commit murder. Big Helen once more testified as a prosecution witness, recounting the same details of the plot and the murder. She also told the jury that at least one other woman had been asked by Loretta to kill Red, but refused.

Asked by Deputy Prosecutor Clelland Hanner (Prosecutor James Hanner's father) why she participated in the murder, Big Helen replied: "'Cause I fell in love with her, Mrs. Stonebraker."

The motive of Big Helen's cohort, the defendant Sigler, was money, the prosecutor told the jury.

The panel deliberated nearly eight hours before returning guilty verdicts on both charges. Judge Dowd sentenced Sigler to sixty years in prison for murder and fifty years on the conspiracy charge. He ruled the sentences should be served concurrently. Like his cousin Loretta, Sigler would be eligible for parole from the Indiana State Prison at Michigan City in about thirty years.

Finally it was Big Helen's turn. She had admitted her part in the conspiracy, and turned state's evidence against her co-conspirators.

According to a plea agreement, the thirty-nine-year-old woman entered a guilty plea in Parke Circuit Court to charges of conspiracy to commit murder and was sentenced by Judge Dowd to a twenty-five-year prison term. She would become eligible for parole in about twelve years. As part of the agreement, the charges of aiding, inducing and causing the murder were dropped by the prosecution.

Both Big Helen and Loretta were sent to the Indiana State Women's Prison in Indianapolis to serve their sentences.

"If there's any trouble it will be on her part, not mine," Big Helen said of her former lover.

CHAPTER TWO

DROWNING OF
THE PREGNANT BRIDE

Darkness had just settled and lights from the city sparkled in golden columns on the placid waters of the Atlantic when the U.S. Coast Guard was first alerted to a tragedy.

Michael Keen, a successful local Fort Lauderdale businessman, tearfully reported that he had just docked his cabin cruiser after an all-day pleasure outing and discovered that his wife was missing. He was afraid she had fallen overboard.

The Coast Guard searched for Lucia Ana "Anita" Lopez Keen with cutters, airplanes and helicopters for four days, but the body of the twenty-two-year-old, Cuban-born beauty was never found.

According to the story blurted out by the

distraught husband that night, and in a subsequent statement to a Broward County Sheriff's Department detective a few weeks later, Keen's wife apparently plunged overboard, unnoticed, while he and a friend were chatting and listening to the radio.

Keen said he had set out on his twenty-three-foot cabin cruiser early Sunday morning, November 15, 1981, with his wife, Anita, and Kenneth J. Shapiro, a close friend, for a day of relaxation on the ocean.

About the time they decided to turn back and head for home, however, Anita went below deck to take a nap. Somehow, unseen by her companions, she must have fallen overboard. Any cries for help would have been drowned-out by the radio, and she wasn't missed until the boat had docked.

Shapiro's recollection of the sad event was similar to his friend's. In a deposition filed several months later, Shapiro recalled that the threesome stood on the bridge chatting and enjoying a soft breeze and the ocean calm for a while before Anita became tired.

He said she went below deck, but emerged a few times while he and Michael sipped at cool drinks and listened to a radio broadcast of a Miami Dolphins football game. Shortly before nightfall, they turned the boat toward Port Everglades at Fort Lauderdale and headed for the waterway that would lead them back home. They assumed that Anita was asleep below.

She wasn't discovered missing until they were almost home. It was then, filled with dread, that they called the Coast Guard, he said. He added that he and Michael spent the rest of the night consoling each other.

"They were very much in love," Shapiro said of the couple.

Anita's loss was doubly tragic because she was four or five months pregnant. It appeared that in one terrible accident the grieving husband had lost both his young bride and his first child.

The couple had been married less than four months, following a modest ceremony in the bride's home in Miami on the previous August 1. Michael had met Anita while she was dating his brother, Patrick, but almost immediately, Patrick had dropped out of the picture and Anita and Michael became an item. Michael was a college graduate and classical pianist; he was handsome, urbane and a successful thirty-three-year-old entrepreneur who was earning some fifty thousand dollars a year in business for himself as an outdoor sign salesman. Anita was bright, charming and an exotic Latin beauty, the daughter of immigrant parents of modest means. She was totally captivated by Michael's sophistication and fast-paced, luxurious lifestyle.

Sheriff's Department investigators had heard much more convincing stories before, and although they couldn't immediately prove that either of the men was lying they decided that the young woman's death deserved a thorough investigation.

Checking up on Michael's background they

learned that he had developed a reputation as a free-swinging, fun-loving bachelor after showing up in the Fort Lauderdale area about four years earlier. He was a playboy who worked hard during the day and liked to make the rounds of the bars and nightclubs at night, spending money freely in the company of beautiful women.

Even the name of his boat, *Foreplay Two,* seemed to hint at an ominously sensual side to his character.

Even more disturbing, they learned that several weeks before the marriage, Michael had taken out two insurance policies totalling $100,000 on Anita's life. The policies carried double indemnity clauses that provided for payment of twice that amount — $200,000 — for death from other than natural causes.

When Michael tried to collect on the policies, however, the insurance companies refused to pay. Because there was no body to prove that his wife was deceased, Anita hadn't been declared legally dead. Shapiro's deposition describing the events he said led up to Anita's disappearance was filed in support of a motion by Michael in Broward Circuit Court as he sought to have Anita declared legally dead so he could collect the money. The motion was rejected by a judge.

Determined to collect, Michael continued to pay the sixty-dollar monthly premiums for the policies on his missing wife in order to keep them current.

Eventually, as the months passed, he relocated to Lake Mary, a small town of about three thousand people near Sanford in east central Florida's Seminole county. He again went into business for himself, this time in nearby Castleberry where he specialized in home improvements, and adopted a new name, Michael Kingston. He also acquired a new girlfriend and began, once again, to consider marriage.

It was almost three years after Anita vanished from the boat before investigators got the break they needed to sort out the real story of how she was lost at sea. And, according to sheriff's detectives, it was Michael's younger brother, Patrick, who was responsible for the breakthrough.

A young man with a history of serious trouble with the law, Patrick had served time in prison after trying to have his wife killed in North Carolina as part of an insurance scheme. After his release from prison, he moved to Florida and eventually settled in the Orlando area.

In 1984 he contacted an investigator with one of the companies that had insured Anita and claimed that he knew the truth about his sister-in-law's disappearance. He said he was willing to speak out if the price was right.

Although the insurance company wouldn't pay for the information, the investigator passed on news of the offer to authorities in Fort Lauderdale.

A few days later Patrick found himself talking about Anita, for free, to Broward County Sheriff's Detective Philip Amabile. It was a story of startling cruelty and greed. According to his brother, Michael had taken his wife twenty miles out into the ocean to die with her unborn child, so that he could collect the insurance money.

Insurance companies and the huge amounts of money they are capable of paying out for losses are notorious targets for the get-rich-quick schemes of con men and hustlers, and they figured prominently in Michael's early retirement plans.

Before he moved to South Florida in the late 1970s, he had been convicted of arson in North Carolina for burning a building there to collect insurance.

And according to Patrick, after settling in the Fort Lauderdale area, Michael began looking for a special kind of young woman: one who was trusting, naive, and from a modest background so that her disappearance would be unlikely to attract much official attention. Anita seemed the perfect victim.

Patrick said his brother offered him half the insurance money if he would help with the murder. He claimed, however, that he had had enough trouble with the law and wanted nothing to do with the scheme. Consequently, Michael approached Shapiro with the plan.

Armed with the new information, police arrested Michael at his office in Castleberry on a warrant charging him with first-degree murder in the death of his wife.

"I consider this the most cold-blooded killing I have ever encountered," Broward County

Sheriff George A. Brescher told the press after the arrest.

Detectives had also been having long talks with Shapiro, and he had a chilling story to tell, completely at odds with the earlier version of Anita's apparent death at sea that he had recounted in the deposition supporting Michael's effort to collect the insurance. Shapiro admitted that he had borrowed thousands of dollars from Michael after moving to Florida in 1978 and going to work for him as a salesman. Michael promised to wipe out the debt if Shapiro helped him get rid of Anita. And, Shapiro said, Michael threatened to kill both him and his aged grandparents in Miami if he refused to cooperate. He was terrified!

Shapiro confessed his part in the plot, and agreed to become a prosecution witness against his friend and employer.

Sheriff Brescher said that Shapiro told them the *Foreplay Two* was bobbing in the ocean some twenty miles at sea when Keen suddenly sneaked up behind his wife and pushed her over the railing. Then, as the desperate woman tried frantically to grab onto the boat and climb back aboard, her husband fought her off, while ordering Shapiro to move the craft away.

The men moved off several hundred yards and slowly circled, waiting for her to drown.

Anita put up a surprisingly spirited fight for life. Despite her advanced pregnancy, she splashed and treaded water for more than an hour, struggling to keep afloat and weakly calling for help. It was beginning to get dark when the men finally lost sight of her, and the macabre deathwatch ended. Michael was convinced his wife was dead, and the men turned the boat toward shore and began the trip back to Port Everglades.

Immediately after his arrest, Michael continued to stick to his original story, but after he was confronted with Shapiro's incriminating statement, he changed his version of the events leading to his wife's death. "I did not physically kill Anita," he told Amabile, and said that he "did not see any strategic reason to confess."

According to his revised account, he admitted that he had discussed murdering his wife for the insurance money with Shapiro, but said that planning and fantasizing were different from actually carrying out a killing.

He claimed that he and Anita were hugging each other and looking out over the water when Shapiro suddenly shoved them both into the ocean.

"You've got to believe me. I never wanted her to die. I wanted that baby. I tried to save her, but she hit her head on the dive platform of the boat," he insisted.

Michael said that Shapiro moved the boat away from them and began circling at about ten or twelve knots, but he managed to swim to it and pull himself onboard. His friend was at the controls, "frozen like a zombie." Anita was nowhere in sight!

In June 1985, more than three-and-one-half

years after his pregnant wife vanished, Michael went on trial in Fort Lauderdale before Broward Circuit Court Judge Patti Englander Henning. Ironically, the presiding judge was also pregnant.

Like Michael's younger brother Patrick, Shapiro was not charged with any crime. He had no criminal record and his presence aboard the boat could have been an important factor in bolstering Michael's story during the police investigation and efforts to collect the insurance benefits. Instead, he became the star witness for the prosecution in his former buddy's first-degree murder trial.

He recounted his version of how he had cooperated passively while Michael stopped the cabin cruiser, placed it in neutral, then descended the ladder, sneaked up behind his unsuspecting wife and suddenly shoved her overboard. And he told of how they circled the struggling woman while she fought to keep afloat, until exhaustion apparently overtook her and she slipped from sight in the gathering dusk.

Shapiro said that his former friend determined to retire by the time he was forty, had concluded that the best way he could accomplish that would be to murder his wife and acquire a large lump-sum insurance settlement, which could be used for investment purposes.

The witness said the actual intention was to watch her slip under the water and drown, so Michael would know beyond a doubt that she was dead and he could make a claim on the insurance policy. Michael would have liked to recover the body, if it had been possible, Shapiro said.

The defendant testified in his own defense and once again blamed the death of his wife on Shapiro. He had covered up the truth behind her death out of misguided loyalty to Shapiro, Michael insisted. He said he believed that Shapiro accidentally lurched into him as he tended to Anita, who was ill, plunging both of them into the ocean.

"She looked like she was seasick or something and might throw up," he said. "I got up and climbed down the ladder, turned toward her and rested my left hand gently on her back. She was leaning over. I leaned over with her and rubbed her tummy," he testified.

Michael said he remembered Anita saying, "I don't feel so good." A moment later he felt a sharp blow to his back, "and I ended up in the water," he told the jury.

His cross-examination by the state led to one of the most dramatic moments of the trial when Prosecutor Rob Carney demanded: "Didn't you tell Kenneth Shapiro how you had tried to beat Patrick's wife to death with a rock in North Carolina in 1973?"

Before the startled witness could reply, Defense Attorney Harry Gulkin was on his feet objecting and calling for a mistrial. Judge Henning denied the request for a mistrial, but barred Carney from further pursuing the explosive subject.

Patrick's former wife had testified in pre-trial proceedings that the two brothers had tried to kill her in 1973 for $200,000 in life insurance benefits, but her testimony was not permitted during the trial itself.

In proclaiming his own client's innocence, Gulkin characterized the prosecution's key witness, Shapiro, as a failure and parasite who depended on Michael for friendship and money. He hated Anita and resented her so much that he pushed both her and Michael overboard, then after coercion by sheriff's detectives, concocted false testimony against his former pal. He argued that Michael could not have shoved Anita overboard in the manner described by Shapiro without hurting himself.

"Kenneth Shapiro is not only a liar, but a very sick young man," Gulkin declared in his summation.

But Prosecutor Carney contended in his final arguments that there was adequate circumstantial evidence to corroborate Shapiro's testimony.

Anita was the perfect girl for Michael, the prosecutor said. "Unfortunately for Anita Lopez, what he was looking for wasn't romance....What he was looking for was a victim, somebody he could insure, somebody he could marry, someone he could marry for money."

After the conclusion of the trial, the seven-man, five-woman jury deliberated for only four hours before returning with a verdict of guilty of first degree murder for Michael Keen.

When the jury reconvened three days later

to consider a recommended sentence, Michael delivered an impassioned two-hour monologue in his own behalf. He blamed his brother, whom he sarcastically referred to as "The Phantom," for his arrest and conviction in his wife's death. The nickname was obviously meant to draw attention to Patrick's absence as a witness, even though he was the first person to accuse him of hatching and carrying out the murder plot.

He and Patrick had a lifelong sibling rivalry, Michael said. He was the achiever; Patrick was the loser. "It was like the Smothers Brothers: 'Mom always liked you best,'" Michael told the jury. Then looking the members of the jury in the eye, Michael asked: "Am I a monster? Am I the scum you think I am?"

His mother, a brother, Kip, and his girlfriend all testified for him as character witnesses. But when the jury foreman announced the panel's recommendation to the court, it was unanimous for a death sentence in Florida's electric chair. According to Florida law, the judge was not bound by the recommendation and could still impose an alternative sentence of life in prison, with no chance of parole for twenty-five years.

Anita's mother, Inez Lopez, had sat in a hallway outside the courtroom, quietly sharing her grief with her husband, Raimundo, during the week-long trial. After the verdict had been announced the heartbroken woman told a reporter that if Keen was executed she and her husband wanted to be present. Keen never telephoned her after Anita vanished, and when she tried to call him, he refused to talk with her, she said.

Speaking through an interpreter, she said, "He not only killed my daughter, but he killed my grandchild. He killed two people."

Predictably, Keen's family and girlfriend were shocked by the verdict. Talking with the press, his girlfriend blamed her sweetheart's conviction on what she claimed were lies and distortions by police, the prosecution — and by Shapiro. Nevertheless, approximately five weeks after the jury returned its guilty verdict and recommendation, Judge Henning sentenced the thirty-seven-year-old businessman to death.

"The facts of this case cry out for the imposition of the death penalty," she said. The judge pointed out that the defendant was motivated by greed to unmercifully take the lives of his new wife and unborn child. "A more heinous, atrocious and cruel act carried out in a more terrifying fashion cannot be imagined by this court nor tolerated by society," she declared.

"The victim was left without any assistance, to tread water for as long as her strength, already being shared with her unborn child, would hold out," she said.

Referring to a defense contention that there was no evidence the victim had been tortured, that she was swimming and had not cried out for help, the judge observed: "If only alive for a brief period of time, surely she was alive long enough to see her newlywed husband watching, and to realize with horror that he was not helping and was the cause of her death.

"Surely she was alive long enough to know the horror that she would never make it to the safety of a shore she could not even see.

"Surely she was alive long enough to know the horror that her unborn child would also go to a watery grave.

"Surely she was alive long enough for the total inky black of night to surround her in the ocean filled with the unknown, filled with horror."

Approximately two years after Michael Keen was transported to death row in the Florida State Prison at Raiford, the Florida Supreme Court overturned his conviction and sentence on grounds of a prosecutor's error. The court ruled that an assistant state attorney improperly raised the defendant's previous criminal history during the 1985 proceeding, and ordered a new trial.

There was a new prosecutor, a new defense attorney and a new jury, but the same judge presided at Keen's second trial. And once again Shapiro was the key witness against his former friend. The jury of eight men and four women heard basically the same story from Shapiro and other witnesses as their predecessors had. They heard how Keen schemed for years to find an unsuspecting woman, marry her, insure her life for a large amount of money, then murder her to collect it so that he could retire young.

Shapiro quoted the defendant, now balding

and with a prison pallor that showed the effects of his two years behind bars, as telling him of the unsuspecting young Miami woman: "Anita is the one."

Keen also took the stand once again, and as he had before, pointed the finger at Shapiro as the real killer.

In closing arguments, Assistant States Attorney Bill Dimitrouleas reminded the jury of testimony that Keen planned to recover his wife's body so he could prove she had drowned, and along with Shapiro circled the struggling woman until darkness closed in, waiting for her to give up.

"He didn't count on Anita fighting so hard for her life and her baby's life," the prosecutor said.

This time it took the jury almost thirteen hours of deliberation, but the verdict was the same: guilty of first-degree murder.

Arguing for the death penalty, Dimitrouleas said, "It's difficult to find a more evil, wicked, atrocious or cruel crime than leaving your pregnant wife ten, fifteen, twenty miles out there to drown as darkness is falling."

However, Defense Attorney, H. Dohn Williams, Jr., pleaded with the jury to reject the death penalty. Life in prison, he said, was a far more severe punishment.

"What could be more of a tortuous existence than to spend the next thirty or forty years incarcerated, knowing what he did?" the attorney asked. "Death would bring an end to that suffering."

Williams also reminded the jury that Shapiro, who was present when Mrs. Keen died, escaped prosecution. And two of the convicted killer's former jailhouse confidantes, a child molester and an armed robber, were released on probation after testifying against him.

The jury deliberated on the penalty less than an hour. Then, as their counterparts in the first trial had done, the new jury recommended death in Florida's electric chair. But this time the recommendation was not unanimous and the jury split seven to five, favoring execution.

In October, 1987, Judge Henning once again sentenced Michael Keen to die in the electric chair for the coldly calculated and cruel murder of his pregnant wife. Keen was returned to Raiford and death row.

Even then, Keen's troubles weren't over. New charges were filed against him, accusing him of conspiracy to commit first-degree murder. A cellmate claimed to authorities that Keen had offered him money to kill Shapiro, so that he couldn't testify against him in the retrial. At this writing those charges are still pending.

CHAPTER THREE

A SECRET LIFE

A bone-chilling late winter rain had rumbled across the West-Missouri farmlands during the night and lumpy black clouds still clinging close to the ground, jealously guarded the last of the pre-dawn darkness, when Clifford Gustin was startled by the blasts of a car horn outside his home.

He was even more surprised when he opened his front door to be confronted with a distraught neighbor, Patricia Prewitt, and four of her five children. A series of livid scratches traced an ugly path horizontally along the pallid flesh of her neck from her Adam's apple to her collarbone, and the woman was hysterical.

As the adults guided the sleepy, shivering youngsters inside the house, the young wife and mother blurted out a horror story: She thought her husband was dead — shot to death by a violent intruder who had somehow entered their house as they were sleeping.

A former law enforcement officer, Gustin telephoned his friend Bill Scott, who was chief-of-police in Holden, a small nearby farming town, and relayed the report of the shooting.

A short time later, guided by a flashlight, the police walked cautiously inside the darkened Prewitt house. After groping their way to the circuit-breaker box where a switch moved to the "on" position restored the lights, they continued upstairs.

Dressed in his night clothes, the body of thirty-five-year-old William E. Prewitt was curled up in a sleeping position on a bed in the master bedroom. Blood from an ugly hole in his right temple had seeped onto the pillow and sheets and there was no question that the man was dead.

Aware of the importance of leaving the crime scene undisturbed, Gustin and Chief Scott carefully avoided touching anything, and left to telephone Johnson County Sheriff Charles Norman.

Soon after, Sheriff Norman had taken charge of the investigation, and along with deputies from his staff was busily looking for signs of an intruder and collecting evidence.

A deputy discovered an empty .22-caliber shell casing in the bedroom, and a single-shot .22 rifle was found stored in a closet just off the kitchen.

Faint fingers of light were beginning to break up the overcast sky, when chief investigator Kevin Hughes of the sheriff's department talked with Mrs. Prewitt in the Gustin home at about 5 A.M. on February 18, 1984.

According to Mrs. Prewitt's story, pieced together from that interview, a later, more extensive and formal statement to authorities, and in subsequent courtroom testimony, the nightmare started after she and her husband joined another couple for a night out.

The Prewitts and their friends shared a barbecue dinner in the town of Pleasant Hill in nearby Cass county, stopped at a bar called the Stumble Inn for beers and then went to the home of the other couple to play video games.

According to Mrs. Prewitt, they returned to their own home late, and she walked out to a pond on their property to check erosion before going to bed.

Sometime later, Mrs. Prewitt related, she was awakened by what she thought was the sound of twin thunderclaps. The next moment she was being yanked out of bed by her hair, and was horrified to see that she was in the grip of a stranger.

The intruder held a knifelike object to her throat while he ripped off her nightclothes and threw her roughly to the floor, she said. While he was fumbling with his belt, she started to cry, and disgusted with her sobs, he grumbled, "I hate it when they cry." Then he disappeared into the gloom, and left.

Still crying, she crawled across the floor

through the darkness on her hands and knees to the bed where she tried to awaken her husband. He was alive, but his breathing was labored and rattled.

Unable to rouse him, she went to check on the children. Finding them all right, she returned to the bedroom and tried again to rouse her husband. Once more she was unsuccessful, so she hurried outside and retrieved a flashlight from the family's pickup truck.

This time, when she returned to the bedroom with a flashlight, she saw blood on the bedding next to her husband.

Mrs. Prewitt said she got the children up, telling them there was a small fire in the house and they had to get out. She got them dressed and downstairs, and sent them to the car — admonishing them to lock the doors — before returning to the bedroom for one last check on her husband. He no longer appeared to be breathing.

Unable to help him, she returned to the car and drove towards Holden to summon help. When she saw lights on at the Gustin house about a mile from her own home, she stopped there.

Asked for a description of the intruder, Mrs. Prewitt said that it was too dark to see him clearly. But she indicated he was of about average size, and spoke in a hoarse whisper. She described him as needing a shave, and smelling like tobacco and motor oil.

She said she had tried to telephone for help

after the attack, but the phone cords were cut.

Hughes confirmed that the lines were cut as Mrs. Prewitt reported. Curiously, however, there was no indication that the phone itself had been disturbed as it might have been if a distraught person had fumbled for it in the dark and tried to make a call. The chief investigator was also curious about the lack of suspicious tire tracks in the driveway just outside the house. Only two sets of tracks were left in the mud there — those made by Mrs. Prewitt's vehicle, and those left by Gustin and Chief Scott when they drove up to the home.

It seemed unlikely that a burglar or rapist would have parked far from the house in such nasty weather, and there were no signs of strange footprints leading to or from the house, in the rain-softened earth.

It had been a good story that the distressed thirty-four-year-old widow delivered, but it wasn't a great one.

Hughes was also aware that a large percentage of the murders committed in North America — some experts believe as much as seventy-five percent — are family related. Every day parents, siblings, or spouses kill each other because of money, lovers, mental instability and quarrels sparked by a dizzying variety of reasons, some of them pathetically petty.

Apparently, Hughes wasn't the only one who had reservations about Mrs. Prewitt's tale of violence and tragedy. Later, during the day of the slaying, Mrs. Gustin heard neighbours theorizing that the widow may have had a lot more to do with her husband's death than she was admitting to.

Nevertheless, it seemed hard to believe that Patty Prewitt would do anything to bring about the death of her husband. For one thing, the couple wasn't wealthy. And running a business and raising five children by herself could be a devastating responsibility for the young widow.

When the woman who had been out with the Prewitts the previous night saw her friend at the Gustin house, Patty appeared to be in shock. Anxious to help the shaken family, Patty's friend went to the Prewitt home to pick up some clothing for them, and as she was leaving she considered gathering up a pair of red boots along with other items. But the boots had been left outside and were wet and muddy, so she decided to leave them, a decision that would later take on surprising importance.

The Prewitts had good neighbors and loyal friends. Since they had first shown up in Holden and gone into the lumber yard business more than seven years earlier, the youthful husband and wife had built reputations as respected citizens and leaders of the community. Patty was friendly and outgoing, and was well liked by the employees as well as the customers at the lumber yard. She had served as president of the local chamber of commerce in 1983, before cutting back on her business and outside work activities to spend more time at home.

Bill was industrious and appeared to be a

competent businessman who knew how to establish goals and accomplish what he set out to do. The children, whose ages ranged from six to fourteen at the time of the family tragedy, were both well-behaved and well-liked at school.

Bill and Patty, who met in the seventh grade, had begun going together when they were seniors in high school. They continued dating after enrolling at Central Missouri State University, and married in 1968 after completing their freshman year.

While Bill continued his education, they lived in Lee's Summit, just outside Ray Town at the southeast edge of Kansas City, Missouri. After he graduated they moved a few miles north, still just outside Kansas City, to the small town of Kearney, where he took his first teaching job.

However, Bill quickly realized that he wasn't cut out to be a teacher, and they moved back to Lee's Summit where he found work he liked better in a lumber yard. In 1976 they bought their own lumber yard business in Holden, and moved to the community a short time later, settling in a farmhouse just north of town.

With a houseful of children to raise and a business they were trying to build, they piled up staggering debts, including family loans, bank loans and money owed to suppliers that amounted to more than $150,000 by 1984.

However, the Prewitts weren't the first couple to go into debt in efforts to get ahead and from most appearances, seemed to have developed into an ideal American family. They were hard working, devoted to their children, took part in school activities, and were respected by their neighbors.

But Sheriff Norman's deputies and investigators from the Missouri Rural Crime Squad, which was called in to help, were uncovering some ugly blemishes that marred the picture of domestic happiness presented to the couple's neighbors. And they were accumulating some unsettling information and clues that seemed to point the finger of guilt at the widow.

Two days after the shooting, sheriff's officers again talked with Mrs. Prewitt. During the marathon interrogation, which lasted a gruelling seventeen hours, holes began to appear in her story and she started making changes in her account. For one thing, after denying there had been problems in her marriage and telling officers that neither she nor her husband were ever involved in extramarital relationships with others, she changed her story. After investigators confronted her with names, she reluctantly admitted that she had carried on affairs with three men.

Mrs. Prewitt told the officers that the trouble in her marriage started in 1974 after she was gang-raped during a business trip she and her husband took to Sedalia in neighboring Pettis county. She said that because her husband still had some business to take care of and she wanted to shop, they agreed to meet in a park near the business district. She got to the park first and was pulled into the bushes and raped by three men who had followed her.

An elderly woman finally came out of a nearby house and frightened the rapists off, Mrs. Prewitt said. Her rescuer took her inside the house and helped her clean up.

She told her interrogators that when she told her husband about the assault, they agreed it would be too embarrassing to let anyone else know what happened. Consequently, the rape was never reported to the police.

Although her husband was sympathetic at first, she said, their relationship gradually changed and he became more distant. Their lovelife suffered, and after he finally stopped making love to her altogether, she turned to other men for affection. Her husband was apparently unaware of her flings with other men, except for one time when he caught her hugging and kissing one of her lovers in a car parked in the Prewitt driveway.

Hughes later testified in court that Mrs. Prewitt admitted meeting the man she was caught with in the car, once a day and sometimes two and three times a day during their approximate four-month affair. Sometimes she had liaisons with two of her lovers on the same day, and they usually made love in her home while her husband was at work and the children were at school. When the officer indicated amazement at her tales of illicit romance, he said that she had replied: "My fire burns hotter than others!"

But she insisted that by the time the shooting occurred, the affairs were a thing of the past. Her romantic relationship with her husband had improved, she said, he had become more attentive to her, they were getting along well, and she hadn't cheated on him for four years or more.

Investigators had also recovered the gun they believed was the death weapon. It wasn't the single-shot weapon found in the home, but a .22-caliber repeater rifle that belonged to the family, and was normally kept with the other in a closet next to the kitchen.

Under Sheriff Norman's direction, officers had launched a small boat on the pond, and began searching the bottom with powerful magnets. The rifle was found in about eleven inches of water, some fifteen feet from the bank. Mud was jammed two-and-one-half inches into the muzzle of the barrel.

The day after the weapon was recovered, the water in the pond was drained off and a footprint was found in the mud at the bottom. The print matched other footprints on the bank of the pond, which carried the same pattern found on the soles of a pair of Mrs. Prewitt's red boots. It was the same pair of petite woman's boots her friend had nearly picked up the day she was gathering up clothing for the family.

The investigation team theorized that the rifle was tossed from the shore into the pond, and stuck barrel down in the mud, so that the stock stood up in the air. The footprints indicated to the officers that someone had walked into the pond to get the gun and pushed it back down into the water so that it would lie flat under the surface.

Ballistics tests confirmed that firing-pin markings on the casing found in the bedroom and test-fired cartridges from the rifle were identical.

Mrs. Prewitt was arrested on charges of capital murder in the slaying of her husband. She was released on $75,000 bail, pending trial. Approximately one month before her trial, moved on venue to Sedalia, Bill Prewitt's body was exhumed so a second autopsy could be performed.

The first autopsy, performed the day of the slaying, indicated that the victim was shot once in the right temple. The pathologist's report indicated the bullet had split and taken two paths through the skull.

Powder burns indicated the weapon was held about three to six inches from Prewitt's head, and he was probably asleep when he was shot.

Ten months after the slaying, however, Dr. James Bridgens, a highly respected Kansas City forensic pathologist, was called into the investigation. He reviewed the autopsy report, photos from the crime scene and x-rays — and then called for another postmortem. It appeared that the victim had been shot twice, not once as previously believed, and that the second shot was fired into his mouth, damaging a front tooth.

The examination following exhumation in part confirmed Dr. Bridgens' suspicions. The victim had been shot twice, but the second shot was fired into the back of his head, not into his mouth.

Dr. Bridgens concluded that the first shot was not immediately fatal, and crime-scene photos which showed blood apparently splattered by the injured man's breathing supported that finding. The second shot, however, severed Prewitt's brain stem, causing an injury that would have halted breathing almost immediately.

The new findings were glaringly inconsistent with Mrs. Prewitt's account of crawling across the floor to her husband after he was shot, listening to his tortured breathing, then returning to him sometime later to find him still struggling for breath.

Johnson County Prosecutor Tom Williams had already announced he would not seek the death penalty for the mother of five, when, still free on bail, Patty Prewitt went on trial in Sedalia before Johnson County Circuit Judge Donald Barnes in April, 1985.

In his opening statement, Williams said that Mrs. Prewitt had talked to three men about her desire to see her husband dead. He promised the jury of nine women and three men that he would prove she killed her husband "for money, for lust." She planned the murder for five years, and bragged that the insurance from her husband's death would make her a wealthy woman, the prosecutor declared.

Mrs. Prewitt's defense was headed by a Kansas City lawyer, Robert Beaird, who quickly made it clear that he would show that an intruder who had invaded Mrs. Prewitt's home in the dark of night was the real killer of her husband.

Beaird talked of the rape of Mrs. Prewitt in the Sedalia park and how it had caused serious problems in the couple's marriage, but claimed that she had been far more successful than her husband in putting the painful experience behind her.

"There was a pain there that he just couldn't live with," Beaird told the jury.

By 1980 the wound had started to heal, however, and they were moving back into their old relationship, the attorney insisted, and he promised Mrs. Prewitt would take the stand to testify.

Witnesses for the state were called first, however, and Dr. Bridgens provided testimony that exposed glaring holes in Mrs. Prewitt's account of the shooting. The pathologist not only pointed out that Prewitt would have stopped breathing almost immediately after he was shot in the back of the head, but also declared it was "highly improbable" that the two wounds could have been inflicted by a gun fired in total darkness, as the defendant contended.

Dr. Bridgens testified that according to the position of the victim's body on the bed it appeared highly unlikely that an intruder could have shot him in the back of the head without awakening Mrs. Prewitt, who told authorities she was sleeping next to her husband. Based on the angle of the projectile when the second shot entered Prewitt's head, whoever fired the rifle would have had to lean over the bed so that the weapon would have been almost on top of anyone sleeping next to the victim.

The witness also testified that based on the

pattern of the superficial cuts on Mrs. Prewitt's throat the morning of the shooting, his expert opinion indicated they were more characteristic of self-inflicted wounds than those made by another person. Asked under cross examination if the injuries could have been inflicted by someone trying to restrain her, he said it was possible that an assailant could have caused the scratches, but not very probable.

The prosecution turned early to the muddy red boots which investigators believed Mrs. Prewitt wore to wade into the pond to push the telltale rifle underwater the morning of the shooting. But during cross-examination, the defense got witnesses to acknowledge that even after the pond was drained a ramp was built across the bottom because the mud was too deep for investigators to walk in. And Sheriff Norman conceded that when the footwear was inspected, there was no mud inside the boots or the eyelets which seemed hardly indicative of the condition of boots used to wade in such deep, soft mud.

Later in the trial, Beaird called one of the Prewitt daughters to the stand and she testified that a few weeks earlier she was with a brother when, wearing her mother's boots, she ventured out on the ice of the shallow pond and fell through.

She said they didn't tell anyone about the mishap because they didn't want to get into trouble.

The girl's testimony offered a handy alternative explanation for the bootprint on the bottom of the pond. But there was to be far more dramatic testimony ahead when Mrs. Prewitt's three ex-lovers were called to the stand.

One of the men testified that he had been Mrs. Prewitt's lover for nearly four years and that their romance had begun in 1975 when they were next-door neighbors living near Lee's Summit. He said that after the Prewitts bought the lumber company and moved to Holden, the affair continued until Mrs. Prewitt decided to end it.

The witness related that Patty had told him that William Prewitt didn't satisfy her sexually, and that once when they were together in her home near Holden she had asked him to kill her husband. She had suggested he set fire to their barn, and shoot Prewitt when he went out to fight the blaze, he testified. He also told the court she had offered him $10,000 to carry out the murder, but he had never believed she was serious and told her it was a crazy idea.

The witness also admitted during cross-examination that he had been in love with her. Although he was married by the time he appeared in court, and claimed to no longer love Patty, he said he had offered to get a divorce and marry her so that he wouldn't have to testify against her, but she turned him down.

The witness, who admitted during cross-examination that he had used heroin, LSD and marijuana, said he and his wife were guests at the Prewitt home two weeks before the murder.

And he said he had fired the .22-caliber single-shot rifle owned by the Prewitts, but not the repeater rifle used in the slaying.

Another of Mrs. Prewitt's lovers confirmed under cross-examination that he had been promised by the authorities that he wouldn't have to testify in court if he made an official statement.

He testified, nevertheless, that he had had sexual relations with Patty Prewitt on three occasions in 1979 before he moved away and the brief affair ended.

During the time they were romantically involved, however, he said she suggested that he help her murder her husband. In return, she offered to help set him up in his own lumber yard business, but he indicated that he hadn't taken her talk seriously.

On cross-examination, the witness acknowledged that he had been once convicted of cattle theft, and was in trouble with police over an assault charge when authorities approached him during the murder investigation. Proceedings in the assault case had been subsequently dropped.

During an approximate four-month affair, Mrs. Prewitt's third ex-lover also claimed to the court that she had talked several times to him about wanting her husband dead.

"She had said that she wished he, Bill, would be killed in a car accident or some type of accident, and that she knew where the gun was and had thought about killing him in his sleep," he related. That witness, too, said he hadn't taken her talk seriously.

When she was called to testify in her own defense, Patty Prewitt denied that she had ever talked to her lovers about killing her husband. Asked by Beaird if she had ever talked to one of her ex-lovers about wanting to see her husband dead, as he had testified earlier, she replied: "No, unless it was in a kidding way …not the way it came across (in testimony)."

When Prosecutor Williams questioned her about her ex-lover's testimony that she told him she wanted to see her husband dead, she shot back: "I don't know what you did to make him say that."

The attractively slender defendant admitted taking lovers to fill the void in her life when the romance dropped out of her marriage following the gang rape she said occurred in Sedalia. She insisted that she and her husband never considered divorce and continued to work well together even after their sexual relationship soured.

"I didn't like what was happening between us, but I never hated Bill," she declared.

"I felt alone, lonely. I needed someone to be nice to me. I needed someone to hold."

Although firmly denying she sought to enlist any of her lovers as accomplices in a murder scheme, she admitted to falsely complaining to them that her husband beat her. She said she lied about the beatings so that her boyfriends would sympathize with her and not think she was a bad woman.

But she firmly denied making the remark attributed to her by former-investigator Hughes about having unusually strong sexual drives, or as he also testified, suggesting during an interrogation that he might find it an interesting experience to take her to dinner.

During more than two hours on the stand, the witness also told of her reaction to what she said were the efforts of her longtime lover and former Lee's Summit neighbor to rekindle the flames of their romance after she had called the affair off.

"He tries to see me alone and says he still loves me. I tell him I don't love him, but he won't listen to me," she told the jury. "He scares me. He's weird!"

Mrs. Prewitt stated that business and personal debts at the time of her husband's death totalled about $170,000. Her defense attorney later pointed out that insurance policies on her husband's life were still considerably less than the couple's debt totals.

During her sometimes tearful testimony, the petite witness told the jury that she had co-operated fully with authorities from the beginning of the investigation because she was anxious to see the killer of her husband brought to justice. She pointed out that she didn't even ask for a lawyer after she was told that she was a suspect and advised of her constitutional rights.

"I thought if you were innocent all you had to do was tell the truth," she said. "I couldn't believe they thought I did it . . . It was all a nightmare."

In Beaird's summation near the conclusion of the four-day trial, her attorney claimed that the police had done shoddy work, and charged that within hours of the slaying, Hughes, the principal investigator, had focused on his client as the suspected killer merely because it offered the most convenient means of accounting for the murder.

Beaird accused authorities of failing to make a serious search for an intruder. He pointed out that two of the Prewitt children testified that they had heard or saw something out of the ordinary in the basement of the family home the night of the slaying. The girl who fell through the ice on the pond said she had heard a noise and seen a light in the basement the night her father was shot. And a younger girl said she had heard something there while her mother was getting her and the other children up to lead them out of the house.

Beaird told the jury that evidence suggested that the man who testified to having been in love with Mrs. Prewitt and offered to divorce his wife and marry her, could have been involved in her husband's death. The defense attorney also noted that the Prewitts had previously complained to police of receiving obscene telephone calls.

He reminded the jury that twenty-five law enforcement officers working on the case were unable to turn up evidence of his client carrying on any outside love affairs for the previous five years, which supported her testimony that her relationship with her husband had improved.

And he recalled for the panel the character

flaws in two of her ex-lovers, one a former drug user and another a once-convicted thief. He complained that investigators had put heavy pressure on the men to co-operate with them, even threatening them with jail if they refused.

The prosecutor agreed in his summation that the ex-lovers of Mrs. Prewitt whom he had called to testify against her were what he termed, "a motley lot." But he reminded the jury that he hadn't selected the men. Patty Prewitt had!

Williams told the jury that Patty's patience, and her husband's insurance, were running out after years of trying to recruit someone to kill him. They were presented with evidence that showed she finally loaded the victim's repeater rifle with five rounds of ammunition, and fired a bullet into his head, the prosecutor said. When that didn't kill him, she fired a second shot.

Her motive was "greed and sexual lust, and had been for years," he said. Williams told the jury that Mrs. Prewitt was after $130,000 in insurance on her husband, and that with him dead she would be free and independent.

The prosecutor derided Mrs. Prewitt's story of an intruder as incredible. "Patty Prewitt admits one falsehood after another," he reminded the panel, "but she expects you to believe her now."

After less than six hours of deliberation, the jury returned a verdict of guilty to capital murder. When the verdict was read by the court clerk, Mrs. Prewitt's children screamed, and were ushered from the courtroom crying and wailing, "no, no, no." Several of the jurors also broke down in tears.

Judge Barnes sentenced Mrs. Prewitt to life in prison, with no possibility of parole for fifty years, the only possible sentence for the crime under Missouri law except the death penalty, which had been waived.

CHAPTER FOUR

THE KILLING
OF THE SHREW

When a dark-haired California beauty and a handsome member of a titled English family who was heir to a fabulously wealthy fortune met and married, it seemed to be the classical conclusion to a fairytale romance.

But Michael Telling wasn't a dashing prince. Nor even a proper English gentleman. He was a miserable, cringing wimp and lifelong weakling with a sad history of severe psychiatric and emotional problems.

And Monika Elizabeth Zumsteg wasn't the breezily innocent, American girl-next-door of Gidget movies. She was a lust-driven bisexual with a history of alcoholism, who developed an insatiable appetite for sex and drugs. She was also a heartless shrew who delighted in humiliating her new husband in front of her friends and lovers with cruel taunts about his sexual inadequacies and inability to fit in.

As second cousin to billionaire Lord Vestey, a member of the family which controls an international meat fortune, and a polo-playing pal of Prince Charles, Michael was born into a life of wealth and privilege. Said to be the second wealthiest family in England, the Vesteys founded their business empire more than a century ago, and as the world's largest retailer of meat, maintained ranches in Argentina, Australia, Brazil, Canada, New Zealand and South Africa as well as a fleet of refrigerated ships and hundreds of butcher shops. Family interests control 250 companies in 27 nations.

Yet, despite the high station in society that seemed to be Michael's birthright, he got off to a rocky start. He was deprived of love, and years after Michael's birth, his father would be recalled in courtroom testimony by an esteemed professor of forensic psychiatry as an allegedly violent alcoholic who chased his pregnant wife with swords.

During Michael's pre-school years, he was raised by a series of governesses in a separate suite from his parents, and was permitted daily visits with his mother, Joyce, of no longer than one hour at a time.

By the age of three, when Michael was already a confirmed diabetic, his mother divorced his father and eventually moved to Australia where she remarried a man named Strong in the ambassadorial service.

When he was four years old Michael, angered by his favorite nanny, erupted into a rage and tossed all of her belongings out of her room.

When he was five, his neighbors were ordering their children not to play with him because one of his favorite pranks was chasing other youngsters and tossing lighted matches at them.

At seven, while attending an exclusive but strict boarding school, and still unable to read, he plunged into a diabetic coma after breaking into the snack shop, stealing and gorging himself on sweets.

Recovered from the diabetic attack, he began startling drivers by running naked into the road, throwing himself down in front of cars, then scampering out of the way at the last moment.

He was exceptionally small for his age, frail, and sickly, and he quickly became identified as such a pathetic misfit that almost none of the other boys at the school would have anything to do with him. He tried, almost always in vain, to buy friends with bribes of candy and other prized possessions.

A former classmate, later recalling the tragic child, said that bullies once made him pay a terrible forfeit in order to be allowed to play in a school game. Michael was forced to roll around in a patch of stinging nettles until he looked like "one huge blister." His body was red and swollen from head to toe, the classmate said. Then the other boys refused to let him play in their game, anyway.

Michael was nine when he smashed a milk bottle over the head of a clergyman's daughter.

He was the same age and known among his schoolmates as "Telling, The Terror," when he set fire to a school staircase one night. The arson was his final prank at the school. After being given a severe paddling, he was expelled.

He once threatened to kill his mother, and she later remembered that when four sharp carving knives were found in his room, "he warned me off with them."

Before he reached his teens, Michael had spent three years in a London psychiatric hospital. After the boarding school and mental hospital, his parents also tried changing his outrageous behavior by sending him to a school for problem kids. He responded with more misbehavior, including a thwarted effort to strangle a pet hamster.

Twice, in 1970 and again in 1974, he unsuccessfully tried to commit suicide with overdoses of sleeping tablets.

Not surprisingly, although he was of average intelligence, Michael did not perform well in his classes. After completing what is roughly equivalent to high school in the U.S. and then failing to qualify for college, he found a job in a factory. Two years later he went to Australia, enrolled in a technical college, then worked at a series of menial jobs in a mens-wear shop, in restaurants and in an auto plant.

When he became twenty-one years old, he began receiving about eighteen hundred dollars in monthly income from a family trust — in addition to credit card accounts and various other bills being paid from the fund — and he dropped out of the work force to indulge himself in travelling and building up collections of guns, motorcycles and expensive electrical gadgetry. He never held another job.

About a year earlier, Michael had met a pretty waitress named Alison Webber, from the Western Australian city of Perth, and they became sweethearts. The couple eventually returned to England, married, bought a home with money from the trust fund and in 1979 became parents of a son they named after his father.

Michael, however, was a less than perfect husband, and his moodiness, emotional immaturity and refusal to accept adult responsibilities hurt the marriage. He was also fond of packing his bags and running off on luxury foreign vacations at the drop of a hat. In 1980 he flew to California to indulge one of his dreams by purchasing a large American-made Harley Davidson motorcycle.

The aimless young husband was in the San Francisco area when through her parents who lived north of the city in Santa Rosa, he met Monika, the oldest of their three children and big sister to teenage twins.

Michael was bowled over by the vibrant California girl's beauty and charm, and she seemed to be equally taken with the handsome Englishman.

He paid his new girlfriend's rent on an apartment, and flew back to England to have a serious talk with his wife. Alison and Michael split up, and Monika traveled to England. As soon as Michael's divorce became final, Monika became the new Mrs. Telling.

On their wedding night in London's posh Hyde Park Hotel, Michael's lovely bride from America refused to sleep with him.

Months later Richard Bluglass, a professor of forensic psychiatry at Birmingham University, and a member of England's Mental Health Review Tribunals, told a courtroom gathering that during a lengthy interview, Michael said Monika had gotten drunk before banning him from her bed. From the day of their marriage, Michael told the psychiatrist, she became aggressive and different from the sweet, charming companion and lover she had been before.

Overnight, the passion Monika had shown in California for the troubled young English blueblood turned from hot to cold. According to the professor's testimony, and to others who knew the couple, Monika also seemed to delight in tormenting and humiliating her husband.

Even before their wedding, Michael told Professor Bluglass, he came downstairs from bed one night and found his twenty-six-year-old sweetheart half-naked on the floor of their sitting room petting with a beautiful neighbor, the wife of an attorney.

After the wedding, Michael complained, they were on a grocery shopping trip when she casually mentioned to him that while he was hospitalized for depression she had taken up with a former Mexican lover. He said she bragged that the ex-boyfriend, who had once helped her with an abortion, was in England.

As soon as the couple settled in a luxury $190,000 country estate called Lambourne House, in the village of Bledlow Ridge, West Wycombe, some thirty miles northwest of London, Monika became a regular on area golf courses, and eventually joined the darts team at a local pub. She also began trying to break into the modeling scene. Despite her attractiveness, however, she was unsuccessful and had to settle for doing some local modeling at a charity fund show in a church hall.

With her modeling ambitions pushed into the background, it wasn't long before she was building a local reputation as a swinger who let nothing stand in the way of good times. The privacy of the Lambourne House location in the rolling Chiltern Hills and its luxurious amenities — a whirlpool bath on the lawn, and a half-finished sauna — made it perfect for parties. And Monika threw plenty of them. Local villagers soon got used to the sound of revelry throughout the summer, with loud music and dancing on the lawn into the early morning hours.

However, if Monika was having a good time, Michael wasn't. She continually belittled his sexual prowess by loudly complaining to friends that she couldn't get "a decent screw" out of him.

According to other stories that circulated, when Monika scampered delightedly across the lawn at other parties to join naked guests in the whirlpool bath, Michael watched quietly from the sidelines, sipping morosely at a drink.

Monika also entertained at more private parties. A dark-haired, twenty-one-year-old coed eventually admitted in open court that she had boozed, smoked pot and made love with Monika in the Tellings' bed. She said that once when she was leaving the house at about nine o'clock in the morning, she met Michael near the door. He had been perfectly polite, and moved his car from the drive so she could get her own vehicle out of its parking place.

Monika and her student lover occasionally got together at the flat of a teenage waitress for pot-smoking sessions. The waitress once spent a weekend at the Telling home, and was embarrassed when Monika taunted Michael in front of her by calling him "a little rich kid" and making fun of his sexual shortcomings.

The waitress later disclosed in court that her American friend had urged her to return to the United States with her as soon as she was divorced from Michael. Monika had bragged that she was only staying with her husband until she could get a big chunk of his money.

Another woman, Cheryl Richardson, who with her husband, Richard, had been close friends with the Tellings since meeting Michael through his interest in CB radios, would be quoted in a London news report as saying she was appalled by a brazenly open sexual pass Monika made at her at the luxury farm home. A mother of three, Mrs. Richardson said she went to Monika's bedroom late one morning to tell her she was making coffee. Monika was naked in the bath, and invited her friend to join her.

Shocked, Mrs. Richardson stammered a refusal and fled. But when she returned a few minutes later expecting to find Monika dressed, the American woman was still nude, and embraced her. Then Monika flopped backwards onto the kingsize bed, and patted it, inviting her friend to join her. Shaken and disgusted, Mrs. Richardson turned on her heels and left.

Another time, Monika was equally frank about her lesbian leanings, and according to Mrs. Richardson's courtroom testimony: "She said that if she screwed me, I would never want another man."

Mrs. Richardson's husband told reporters that he often dropped by the couple's house in the morning, and was used to being greeted by a parade of scantily dressed, young women. One morning a dark-skinned beauty wearing only a see-through nightie walked into the kitchen where he was sitting with Michael and visited for a few minutes. As soon as she left, Michael sadly explained that the girl had shared Monika's bed as a special guest, while he had to sleep on a camp bed in his radio room.

Richardson said Monika seemed amused at his inability to take his eyes off the lightly clad girl, and asked him if he would like to join them in a three-in-the-bed frolic. He said he firmly rejected the offer.

Another time Monika took a torrid vacation trip to Austria with the woman friend she was caught frolicking on the floor with before her marriage. When Michael showed up with money for his wife, her lover became bitchy and Monika ordered him to get out. Michael said that Monika later taunted him by bragging that her lover took sexy nude pictures of her in a bathtub.

Michael fought back ineffectively. He admitted hitting Monika at least four times, but she was the stronger personality, and with her sharp tongue and intimate knowledge of his weaknesses, she always came out the winner. She made his life miserable, nagging him when he drove, and refusing to allow him to have a dog when he wanted one. She turned him in to the police after discovering an arsenal of guns — which are carefully restricted and controlled in England — in their home. And she trained her cockatoo to say: "Piss off, Michael."

Monika's favorite breakfast at Lambourne House was Benedictine and orange juice. The morning drink was usually followed up with a half-bottle of vodka each day.

She cooked only one meal at the house in the almost year and a half that she and Michael lived together there, and the only work she took any interest in was tending her marijuana plants, Michael complained.

He further claimed she tried to stab him twice, run him down with a car, attacked him with a whip, went after him with her sharp fingernails, and once she threw his insulin outside.

Michael tried to find relief in his hobbies and expensive toys, watching television, playing records, tooling around the quiet Chiltern Hills roads and lanes on his powerful motorcycle, and spending hours with his CB radio. His favorite CB identification handles were "Chief Inspector" and "Snake Radio 99."

At the time CBs were extremely popular and Michael made friends over the radio with a forty-four-year-old housewife and mother of three, June Ginnette. Mrs. Ginnette, who used a variety of CB handles, including "Night Nurse," "Pornographic Princess," and "Naughty Nun," became the concerned confidante and caring mother figure Michael had never had.

He poured out his heart to Night Nurse, telling her horror stories about his love-hate relationship with the American wife he said was a cocaine-snorting, pot-smoking, lust-mad bisexual sadist who was turning his life into a living hell. Michael whined that his wife delighted in making him miserable, and was so crazed for constant sex that she drove her gleaming white Pontiac Firebird on regular pub crawls looking for lovers, while carrying a handgun and a vibrator inside her handbag.

At one of their barbecue parties, he told his CB friend, Monika humiliated him by telling their guests what a lovely lapdog he was. "But he's no good in bed," Michael quoted Monika as saying, before holding up her little finger and sneering, "It's only this size."

As sympathetic as she was, Night Nurse was helpless to do anything more than commiserate with her friend. Mrs. Ginnette became convinced that Michael's wife was trying to drive him into a mental hospital, so she could gain control of his money. By that time Michael's annual income from the trust had mushroomed to about $375,000.

Finally Michael had had all of the abuse he could take. He left a handwritten note for Monika, explaining that he couldn't bear to live with her any longer, and was leaving. He advised her that he had made financial arrangements with his attorney for her support. Then Michael cleaned out much of the furniture, and fled to Australia.

Monika simply fled into the arms of a new, and virile lover.

In an exclusive interview with London's *Sunday Mirror*, Joe Stennings, a handsome thirty-one-year-old painter and decorator, recalled Monika as nothing at all like the shrewish, sadistic lesbian others had painted her. Instead, he insisted, he found her sensitive, and "an innocent sort of girl."

Stennings said he was a friend of the couple during the tormented final year of their marriage, and ran into Monika at a pub shortly after Michael flew to Australia. Monika offered to drive him home in her Firebird, and invited him into her house for coffee.

There, Stennings said, she told him her troubles, and before long they had begun to kiss. Then Monika invited him to stay overnight. Stennings recalled that they left their coffee cups on a table next to a photograph of Michael and Monika, as they walked upstairs to the bedroom.

Stennings said they also made love in her bedroom the next night, and he was thinking seriously about building a future with her when Michael returned.

Michael had instructed his lawyer to initiate divorce proceedings, but became concerned when he heard that Monika had been depressed since his departure for Australia and was also worried about some impending dental surgery. So he returned to London, and called his wife, asking her to meet him at the Hyde Park Hotel where they spent their honeymoon.

At the hotel, Michael tried to rekindle their broken romance, and presented his wife with an expensive diamond necklace. He agreed to her demand that he seek psychiatric help, and they returned together to their home.

One day while the troubled couple was sitting in the house with Stennings, Monika suddenly turned to her ex-lover and said: "When he blows my head off one day, you will be able to tell the papers how Lord Vestey's cousin shot me."

Her remark would be remembered months later for its chilling and prophetic accuracy.

Although Michael never indicated that he suspected Monika had carried on an affair with their friend while he was in Australia, the quarrels, the badgering, and the unhappiness, continued just as before.

In March, 1982, four days after the second honeymoon at the Hyde Park, Michael was preparing to comply with his psychiatrist's recommendation that he enter a mental hospital.

According to his account, Monika was in a particularly nasty, nagging mood. She followed him everywhere he went, constantly carping at him to leave for the hospital so that she could get on with her life.

Michael claimed that he left his wife in one room and went to another room where he grabbed a new high-powered Marlin .303 hunting rifle he had purchased on his Australia trip.

Returning to his wife, he leaned the weapon against the wall. A moment later, Monika charged toward him as he stood in a doorway between the lounge and the kitchen. According to his story, he was afraid that she was going to attack him, so he picked up the rifle, and shot her — three times.

Monika was killed almost instantly. One bullet struck her in the throat, two others slammed into her chest.

Michael slumped into a kitchen chair, and stared at the wall. Then he vomited. Trembling uncontrollably, he began to cry, and dropping to his knees, kissed Monika, whispering that he was sorry.

He moved the body to a spare bedroom, and placed it on a camp bed. He returned to it every day, carrying in morning tea and kissing the cold lips while apologizing for hurting her.

Michael told friends and neighbors that he and Monika had separated after all, and she had returned to the United States. The story appeared plausible. Everyone who knew them there was aware of their stormy relationship,

and Monika had told more than one confidante that she was thinking of leaving her weak,
unstable husband, and flying back to California.

Nine days after Monika's death, Michael
brought home another CB chum who used
the code name "Chanel" and tried, unsuccessfully, to make love to her, while the decomposing body of his dead wife lay only a few
feet away.

His new lover was the mother of two, and
started seeing him after splitting up with her
husband about the same time Monika vanished.
They began spending at least part of every
day together, and the thirty-four-year-old
woman listened patiently while he complained
of the terrible treatment he said he had suffered
at his wife's hands. He talked grandly of being
a member of the SAS, the Special Armed
Service that is Britain's elite terrorist-busting
commando unit. He also hinted that he had
been with Britain's armed forces in the Falkland
Islands during the brief military clash with
Argentina. She didn't believe the war stories.
But she did believe that his wife had left him.

She also agreed to accept expensive gifts that
he showered on her including a silver fox coat
he had once given to Monika who had thrown
it back at him. "He craved affection," Michael's
girlfriend later recounted in court. "He tried
to make love to me but failed. He felt humiliated." The affair soon ran its course, but when
they broke up the parting was friendly.

Michael now moved the body of his dead
wife to a cubicle, propping the corpse up against

a wall, in the unfinished garden sauna, which was in a building several yards from the main house. He began seeing an attractive thirty-nine-year-old divorcée, who would later remember him as "eccentric" and as a man who idolized his wife. She also remembered him as a fitful lover, who was gentle and caring, with normal sexual practices, but who was sometimes unable or unready to make love.

A few months after Monika had reportedly returned to America, Michael's first wife, Alison, and five-year-old son, visited him at Lambourne House. The mother and son were blissfully unaware of the horror in the garden sauna only a few yards away.

In September, more than five months after he had murdered his wife, Michael realized that he had to find a way to permanently dispose of the body because officials with the Vestey Trust had decided that the house should be redecorated. So he hired a van, wrapped the corpse in motorcycle covers, and after announcing to friends that he was going on a fishing trip, drove his grisly cargo some one hundred and fifty miles southwest to county Devon. He stopped once for coffee when the odor from the decaying corpse drove him from the van. At the top of a hill a few miles outside the historic city of Exeter along the River Thames, he stopped again — and dumped Monika's body at the edge of the Exeter Forest. Before leaving, he hacked off her head with an ax he had brought with him. He carefully wrapped the head in plastic and returned home, where he stored the bizarre package in the trunk of a mini-car in his garage.

The night after Michael dumped Monika's body in the woods outside Exeter, he slept with his divorcée girlfriend, who like his other sweetheart, never suspected that he hadn't told the truth about his wife leaving him to return to the United States.

However, Michael had already told the truth about Monika's absence to at least one trusted friend, but he wasn't believed. He and Mrs. Richardson, who helped him out as a housekeeper, were returning to the country estate from a shopping trip one day when he blurted out that he had murdered his wife.

Mrs. Richardson later recalled that she was certain that he was joking, even though he insisted it was true and said, "the body was stinking in the sauna." It wasn't many weeks before she had occasion to change her mind about Michael's truthfulness.

A motorist driving between Exeter and the popular resort at Torbay had been desperately seeking an isolated stretch of road for several miles when he pulled his car to a stop at the top of Hadon Hill, stepped out and hurried to the edge of the woods to answer a call of nature.

Moments later he found himself struggling to keep from vomiting as he gazed in horror at a ghastly, decomposing corpse propped grotesquely in a sitting position against a tree. The remains appeared to be those of a young woman. There was no head on the body, and a swarm of insects clustered over the torn and putrefying flesh of the neck.

Although there were indications the corpse had been in the glade only a few days, the advanced state of decomposition indicated the victim had been dead much longer than that — months perhaps.

Pathologists quickly determined that the headless corpse was that of a slender young woman, about five feet tall, who was between twenty and thirty years of age. There was no evidence of sexual assault.

Police, using dogs, had searched the glade and the nearby roadway, but were unable to locate either a murder weapon, or the victim's missing head. Nearly a half-ton of soil was sifted, but investigators produced only a clump of hair that was stiff with blood, along with some teeth and bone chips.

The clues offering the most potential for identifying the body appeared to be her blood-stained clothing. The ghoulish torso was dressed in a pair of scanty, salmon-pink silk shorts made in Thailand and a white T-shirt with the words, "Souvenir du Maroc" printed on it in English and a picture of a dromedary, with Arabic writing under it.

The T-shirt with the reference to Morocco led to some speculation by police and press theorists that the unfortunate young woman might have been mixed-up in the West Country's revived smuggling or drug trade, perhaps as a courier.

Others wondered if she could have been a hooker who got into trouble for stealing from the wrong John, or who was murdered after angering her pimp.

Still others speculated that she could have been just one more unfortunate young woman who left a pub with the wrong date, or hitched a ride with the wrong motorist and ended up dead in the glade after an unsuccessful rape attempt.

Descriptions of the woman and of the distinctive clothing she was wearing were distributed to police departments and to the news media throughout the United Kingdom. The anxious queries of dozens of worried parents, husbands and boyfriends who feared the headless corpse might be someone they loved, were meticulously checked out by investigators. Eventually police cleared away more than seventy missing persons cases, as a result of their widespread inquiry into the bewildering enigma. But for three days the identity of the headless corpse in the glade remained a mystery despite painstaking police work and massive publicity.

Mrs. Richardson was at Lambourne House when a television newscaster announced hours after the discovery that the headless body of a young woman had been found in England's West Country near Exeter. The newscaster was still talking when Michael rushed from the room, staggered into the bathroom and began vomiting.

Mrs. Richardson knew that Michael was a diabetic and hadn't been eating well. She reasoned that his medical condition and lack of food had made him sick. But the nagging memory of Michael's strange confession about killing his wife remained locked in the back of her mind.

Three days later Mrs. Richardson reluctantly went to the police with her suspicions after reading an account of the effort to identify the mysterious headless corpse. The news story carried a precise description of the victim's clothing, and Mrs. Richardson recognized the T-shirt as being identical to a garment that Monika owned. Investigators then checked the teeth found near the body with Monika's dental records. The results were positive. The dead woman dumped in the West Country woods was Michael Telling's twenty-seven-year-old American wife, Monika.

After warning neighbors away because there might be a siege, armed policemen descended on Lambourne House. Michael surrendered peacefully, however, and was led away by several officers for questioning. The police opened the locked trunk of the mini-car, and retrieved the missing head — still wrapped in the plastic bag.

Almost immediately after his apprehension, Michael asked if he could be released on bail. Advised that he could not, he readily admitted to the murder of his wife.

"There you are, I have confessed. I knew you would want a confession," he told a startled police inspector. Then, in a curious statement that indicated he was more concerned at the moment for his two Alsatians than about himself, he asked: "Will you promise to look after my dogs, please? . . . I suppose I'll be in prison thirty, forty or fifty years."

In a rambling six-hour statement, Michael recounted his tale of abuse and humiliation at the hands of his wife, and described what he said were her drinking, drug and sex binges.

"There were one hundred and one reasons," he said of his motive for the slaying. ". . . She kept pushing me, I don't mean she pushed me over. I just snapped at the end . . . I don't mean just nagging, she was horrible in most ways. But it didn't justify killing. What can justify killing?"

Trumpeted in the scandal-loving national press as "The Case of the Headless Corpse," Michael Telling's trial in the Exeter Crown Court was one of the most sensational in modern British criminal history.

When asked to plead to the charge, the short, stocky, thirty-four-year-old defendant responded: "My Lord, not guilty to murder but guilty to manslaughter by reason of diminished responsibility." This plea was not accepted.

Prosecutor Alan Rawley told the jury, which included five women, "It seems his wife was a difficult young woman. It seems that she did use drugs. It seems she was bisexual and it seems that she did belittle him."

He also conceded that Michael had suffered from mental problems and could even have been suffering from some form of mental illness when Monika was slain.

The prosecutor pointed out, however, that Michael had shown cunning, intelligence and a knowledgeable desire to protect himself by his efforts to cover up the crime.

He had conjured up the story about Monika leaving him and returning to the United States, a handy and believable explanation for her sudden absence.

On the evening of her murder, he used her automatic teller card, and continued doing so until the account was almost empty, presumably to give the impression she was still alive.

He paid a private detective to investigate her disappearance.

He broke the murder weapon up and tossed the pieces into a river.

He successfully hid the body for months, first inside his house, then inside the sauna in the outbuilding, to escape detection.

He called in workmen to clean the carpets inside the house to rid the crime scene of bloodstains and other possible evidence of the shooting. And he had an electrical air freshener installed to air out the sauna, after removing Monika's decaying corpse more than five months from the day she was killed.

He drove the body more than one hundred miles from his home to dispose of it in a secluded woods, then chopped off the head to prevent identification and returned with it to his home. He even stuffed the skull with fishing maggots in a coolly calculated move to speed up decomposition.

And Dr. John Hamilton, medical director of England's Broadmoor Prison, who interviewed

Michael at the Exeter jail, testified that the defendant admitted to him that he had decided to murder Monika during their weekend reconciliation meeting at the Hyde Park hotel.

Dr. Hamilton also pointed to Michael's firing three shots into his wife, instead of one, as providing a strong indication of intent. "If it had been an impulsive heat-of-the-moment action, the firing of the first shot might well have brought him to his senses," Dr. Hamilton testified.

"But this cocking of the rifle twice and the firing of the three shots again underlines to me the cold-blooded, calculated way in which he killed her."

Dr. Hamilton observed that throughout their interview, Michael had spent a great deal of time trying to persuade him that Monika had provoked the murder, "and that he was not in any way responsible for his actions."

Dr. Hamilton said he was convinced that Michael was sane. "I believe that although he did have an abnormality of mind, this was not such an abnormality as to have substantially impaired his mental responsibility for his acts," the doctor declared.

Some investigators suggested the case might never have been solved if Mrs. Richardson hadn't recognized the description of Monika's shirt, recalled Michael's startling confession, and notified authorities.

The defense called a parade of witnesses to testify about Monika's drinking and drug abuse, her outrageous sexual romps, and the humiliation she publicly and privately heaped on her husband. Their testimony, as well as descriptions by both the prosecution and the defense, was so damning and critical of the dead woman that during the summing-up at the end of the nine-day trial, Justice Sheldon cautioned the jury to remember that Monika was not alive to answer the attacks on her character.

At many times in the trial it had, indeed appeared as if Monika, not Michael, was on trial. But it was Michael who was convicted.

There is no death penalty in the United Kingdom, but Michael closed his eyes and bowed his head in apparent relief when the jury cleared him of murder and returned a verdict of manslaughter, on the grounds of diminished responsibility. The conviction matched the plea earlier rejected by the court.

Michael winced, however, when the judge refused his attorney's plea for a sentence of fixed length. And he trembled perceptively and wiped tears from his eyes as the judge peered down at him and soberly advised: "In all the circumstances, I have no alternative but to pass a sentence of life imprisonment on you."

The judge added that it appeared Michael had "matured very little from the profoundly disturbed little boy you were. You have little or no greater ability now than then to control your impulses and emotions and the prognosis for the future is bleak," he said.

Justice Sheldon declared that it would be up to those responsible for Michael's custody to decide when, if ever, it was safe and proper to permit his release.

CHAPTER FIVE

THE CHAMELEON KILLER

If anyone ever seemed destined for the comfortable anonymity that comes with the role and responsibilities of an average American housewife, it was Audrey Marie Hilley.

She had a devoted, hard-working husband, two well-behaved, loyal children, loving and proud parents, and the respect of her peers in the community where she had grown up and prospered.

Marie, as she preferred to be called, was one of those fortunate women who, in adulthood, somehow managed to retain an aura of innocent femininity that attracted men and instinctively made them want to protect her. She was petite, with an impish grin, and had an infectious vitality that made people — especially men — feel good just by being around her.

To most of the people in Anniston, Alabama, who knew her she seemed to be sweet, polite, industrious, faithful to her employers, and strongly committed to her family.

But Marie had a sinister other self that was as selfish and deadly as a black widow spider. When the dark passions that smoldered within the soul of the brown-haired, green-eyed homemaker finally surfaced, they led her to strike out in perplexing and violent attacks on the very people who loved her most. And before she was finally brought to justice, she had led the FBI, the police and other law enforcement authorities on a bizarre five-year manhunt that would rival the imagination of the country's best fiction writers.

For the first four decades of Marie's life, she seemed about the closest thing there was to perfection among any of the working-class women she had grown up with in the Calhoun county-seat town of 31,000 in Northeast Alabama.

In addition to being the closest town of any size to the sprawling Fort McClellan Army Base and hosting the Anniston Army Depot, the southern city is known for its iron foundries and textile mills. When Marie was born to Huey and Lucille Frazier during the early years of the Great Depression, her parents both worked at the textile mills and were living in the tiny mill town of Blue Mountain, snuggled close against the western edge of Anniston.

Many of Marie's school friends followed their parents into the mills and foundries. But some of the girls found clerking jobs in local stores and supermarkets, and even more of the boys went into the military service, either through enlistment or the draft.

Redheaded Frank Alfred Hilley was one of those who enlisted in the Navy a short time after finishing high school. Frank was friendly, easygoing and got along well with his fellow sailors, but as soon as he got his first duty assignment — on the 212-square-mile island of Guam in the Western Pacific — he knew that his enlistment was going to turn out to be a very long four years.

Frank was in love with pretty, vivacious Marie Frazier. He had been dating her since he was sixteen and she was twelve. A few months after he arrived on the island, he was given leave, and promptly flew home to marry Marie. She was only seventeen. While Frank finished his Guam tour of duty, his young bride completed her high school education and then went on to secretarial school.

After Frank's Navy tour was over, the couple settled in Anniston where he went to work as a shipping clerk at the same foundry where his father worked, and Marie found a job as secretary for a local attorney.

Their first child, Michael, was born in 1952. More than seven years later, a daughter, Carol Marie, was born. Frank was loving and kind to his wife and children, and Marie was a neat and dedicated homemaker. It seemed to neighbors they were a model family.

The only obvious problem was Marie's weakness for shopping. She just couldn't stop buying things. She bought things she didn't need for the house, she bought things for the kids, for Frank, and for herself. She loved clothes, and her closets were stuffed with them. Consequently, no matter how hard she and Frank worked — he had become a supervisor, and she an executive secretary — they slid deeper and deeper into debt. Marie began hiding bills from her husband. She even got her own post office box, so her bills would be sent there and not to their home where Frank would see them.

Other problems also began to trouble Frank. Small items began to disappear mysteriously from the house. Even more disturbing, he started finding letters that seemed to have been written to Marie from another man. She claimed, however, that she couldn't understand where the notes came from and insisted that she wasn't involved in a back-door romance.

Then, as he was still puzzling over the petty thefts and baffling letters, Frank got sick.

He had always been fit and healthy, a man who seemed to be almost as devoted to hard work as to his family. But suddenly he felt as weak as a baby, and he hurt so badly he could hardly stand it. At first he thought the agonizing pains that ripped through his stomach were merely cramps. But when the over-the-counter remedies he tried failed to relieve the pain, he went to the doctor and had a thorough checkup. The extensive tests he underwent indicated he was healthy, so Frank returned home, looking forward to resuming a normal life.

However, the pain became worse. It wasn't long, in fact, before he couldn't work at all, and was constantly so doubled over in agony that he could hardly shuffle from one room in the house to another. After a few weeks, he was admitted to a hospital. Doctors diagnosed his illness as hepatitis. Then his kidneys failed. The once robust and energetic forty-five-year-old was now a physical wreck and family members had serious fears for his life. Ever the devoted and loving wife, Marie was by his bedside constantly.

Despite Marie's solicitous attention and the most determined efforts of his doctors, a few months after he had first noticed the enigmatic stomach pains, Frank Hilley died. An autopsy, which Marie consented to, indicated that Frank had succumbed to infectious hepatitis.

Suddenly Marie was a young widow with a teenage daughter at home, a heavily mortgaged house and a mountain of debts. (Her son Mike had married.) Frank left a life insurance policy for only $31,000, but ignoring her shaky financial position, Marie went on a spending spree as soon as the insurance money was in her hands. She bought a motorcycle, a television, and a new wardrobe for herself, a car for Carol and home appliances for Mike and his bride.

The curious thefts from the house that had started while Frank was alive, continued to plague Marie and her daughter. And a few months after her husband's death, Marie began to find anonymous notes around the house carrying printed threats to herself and to her daughter. Then a neighbor who lived next door began to find notes with similar threats.

Mike and his wife moved in with his mother and sister. A short time later, Mike's wife, who was pregnant, became violently ill and lost her baby. Soon after, the young couple found a place of their own and moved out of Marie's house.

Then the house caught fire. Damage was severe and Marie filed a lawsuit against the Alabama Gas Company, which she blamed for the fire, but lost it. Nevertheless, she collected insurance, which paid for repairs.

(Later, a couple of other less serious fires damaged homes Marie was living in and destroyed Carol's car.)

Marie also began to get into trouble for bad checks she wrote to finance her shopping sprees, and to bail her out of her deepening financial difficulties when creditors became too persistent.

Her mother, who was her favorite shopping companion, had lost a breast to cancer and because she was still seriously ill and a widow, Mrs. Frazier moved in with Marie. She began to get worse. Just as she had been to Frank, Marie was a caring and seemingly loving nurse to her mother, even learning to administer the shots prescribed to control her patient's pain. However, Mrs. Frazier died in January 1977, leaving a modest burial policy of $600 to Marie.

As the burglaries and other harrassment at her house continued, Marie became expert at filing insurance claims for stolen items. When the police were finally notified and began investigating, one of the detectives got to know her so well that he would occasionally have a cup of coffee and some of her home-baked pastries with her. He also began to have stomach troubles, along with two of the neighborhood children who sometimes sampled Marie's culinary delights.

At one time police were hearing almost daily from Marie with complaints about threatening telephone calls, mysterious notes, prowlers or vandalism. When they arranged to have tracing equipment attached to her telephone to track the threatening calls, the calls immediately stopped. Investigators began to suspect that Marie was playing games with them and started to quietly disengage themselves from the troubled widow.

Marie had been restless since Frank's death and moved around a lot, at one time leaving Alabama altogether and moving to Florida, where she and her daughter lived for a while with Mike and his wife. At various times creditors had repossessed furniture and cars from Marie, and they were again hot on her trail when she left Anniston.

Then Marie and Carol moved back to Alabama and lived with Frank's mother, Carrie Hilley, for a while, and the elder Mrs. Hilley's health started to deteriorate. Marie, meanwhile, was acting unusually strange even for her, and insisted on sleeping on a couch with a crowbar underneath and a handgun within easy reach on a nearby mantle.

Then Carol got sick. Petite, like her mother, Carol had always been active and healthy, but now, barely four years after her father's anguishing death, she began to exhibit the same torturous pains and other symptoms he had had. She doubled over with devastatingly painful stomach cramps, and underwent brutal bouts of nausea and vomiting.

Less than a year before Carol became ill, Marie had purchased a $25,000 insurance policy on her. The teenager's mother was the only beneficiary.

Carol was taken to her doctor, made trips to the hospital emergency room, and was finally admitted to a hospital, where she seemed to get even worse. She had trouble controlling her legs and arms, and they hurt terribly. Although doctors tried everything they could think of to help, and she had fine nursing care, she didn't respond well to treatment. Her mother camped at her bedside, showering her with attention, and couldn't have been more solicitous. As Carol had trouble keeping normal food down, Marie even bought baby food and fed it to her.

Thereafter and for several months, Carol was in and out of hospitals, steadily losing weight, and growing progressively weaker and more desperate over the strange malady that was afflicting her. Marie continued to be solicitous, cooking for her daughter and bringing in her favorite foods from sandwich shops and restaurants. But it seemed like the times Carol was the sickest were just after her mother had given her something to eat.

Marie continued to care for her like a mother hen, however, even during a brief period when Carol tried to make it on her own in a modest apartment she had rented. Carol's mother would go to the apartment and insist that she eat. Marie even bought new furniture for Carol's apartment, but paid for it with a bad check.

Once Marie gave Carol a shot of a milky-white fluid, claiming it would ease the girl's nausea, but it didn't help.

After Carol had been hospitalized four times in Anniston, Marie took her to a Birmingham psychiatrist. On the doctor's advice, Carol was admitted to the psychiatric ward of a hospital there, as it seemed possible that Carol's troubles could be psychosomatic.

By that time the young woman was in ghastly shape. The muscles in her limbs wouldn't work correctly, and she was losing all feeling in her hands and feet. She could hardly walk, or stand, and even her eyesight was blurring.

Secretly, without the knowledge of hospital personnel, Marie gave her daughter more shots, explaining to the weak and desperately frightened teenager that it was medicine to help her.

Shortly after, doctors began to suspect that Carol's troubles might not be psychosomatic after all, and Marie was advised that Carol might be suffering from lead poisoning or poisoning from some other metal.

Over the objections of a doctor, Marie checked her daughter out of the hospital. The next day she had Carol admitted to another Birmingham hospital. A physician there, who became suspicious after learning of Marie's behavior the day before, talked with Carol's former doctor at the first hospital and was told of the signs of metal poisoning. Carol was submitted to an exhausting round of new tests for evidence of poisoning.

Thin white lines were found under her fingernails — damning, almost sure-fire evidence of arsenic accumulation. Arsenic was found in her urine, and in her hair. Her system was saturated with deadly toxins. The tests disclosed that the accumulation had been built up over several months, so long that it was feared the delicate nerves and muscles in Carol's arms and legs might have been irreversibly damaged.

While doctors began the frantic effort to restore Carol's health, law enforcement authorities in Anniston began taking another look at Frank Hilley's death — and at the death of his mother-in-law. They learned that the symptoms of Frank's illness were disquietingly similar to those suffered by his daughter, and despite Mrs. Frazier's history of cancer, her death while living with her daughter also seemed disturbingly suspicious.

Meanwhile, two Birmingham policemen arrested Marie in the waiting room of the hospital where her daughter was being treated for arsenic poisoning. The widow had been named on two charges of passing worthless checks, one for the furniture she had purchased for Carol's apartment. Police had received complaints of other bad checks she had reportedly written on accounts in Alabama and Florida but the two Birmingham counts were sufficient to hold her, while she was being investigated for far more serious crimes.

She was in jail in Anniston when Calhoun County Coroner Ralph Phillips asked her permission to have Frank's body exhumed. Marie readily agreed, adding that she had nothing to fear from an examination of her late husband's remains.

The cadaver was sent to the Alabama State Toxicology Laboratory in Birmingham. Four years after burial, it was amazingly well preserved.

Arsenic remains in the body long after death, and when traces are sought by a skilled pathologist, it is easily identified during post-mortem examinations. When the deadly poison is ingested over a long period of time, it also functions as a preservative, inhibiting deterioration of body tissue. At one time, in fact, the substance was used in embalming fluid. Its use was eventually outlawed because its presence made it impossible after a body was prepared for burial to determine if arsenic poisoning had occurred.

Toxicologists determined that Frank's body contained extremely high levels of arsenic.

A few hours before they announced their findings, authorities in Anniston charged Marie with the attempted murder of her daughter Carol.

A day later, the remains of Mrs. Frazier were exhumed, and pathologists found large amounts of arsenic in her hair and liver. Although Marie's mother had died of cancer, investigators were aware that arsenic can act as a strong carcinogen. They also knew that one reason arsenic is so often selected as a murder weapon is its ability, when administered in small doses over an extended period of time, to produce symptoms that closely mimic other illnesses such as severe viral infections and hepatitis. It has even been mistaken for tuberculosis.

Arsenic is the great pretender of poisons and through its long history as a medium of murder, it has had special appeal for the female killer, anxious to do away with a husband, lover, parent, or child. It ranks with strychnine and cyanide as among the most toxic of all poisons, and can be easily administered repeatedly over a long period of time by a trusted housewife, who cooks and serves the family meals and nurses the ill.

Carrie Hilley's failing health and recurring stomach upsets had resulted in her hospitalization again at about the time that Marie was arrested. She died soon after, of a fast spreading cancer, and an autopsy disclosed high levels of arsenic in her liver.

Despite the desperate efforts of police and prosecutors to keep Marie in jail, and reports of her boasts to fellow inmates that if she ever got out she would immediately head for California, Marie was released on bail. Using aliases, she registered in a Birmingham motel, then switched to another motel in Homewood, Alabama. A few days later she vanished.

Clothing was found scattered around the motel room and a note indicating she had been kidnapped had been left on a table. Marie had complained to her attorneys that she was afraid of members of Frank's family, but the Anniston police remarked that the note appeared to have been authored by someone trying to disguise his or her handwriting.

The day after Marie vanished from the motel room, the home of one of her relatives was burglarized, and women's clothing, savings bonds and a car were taken. Another note was found in the burglarized house, warning the owners not to notify police or they would be burned out. The handwriting in the note was remarkably similar to that of the note left at the motel.

The stolen car was found abandoned at a bus station in Marietta, Georgia. As the fugitive had crossed state lines, the FBI could now enter the case.

But the notorious alleged poisoner was a fugitive for four years. Her disappearance marked the beginning of one of the most bizarre masquerades in the history of American crime.

Retracing her steps much later, law enforcement authorities learned that Marie had apparently traveled to Fort Lauderdale, Florida where she met John Homan.

Homan owned his own boat-building company, and like the late Frank Hilley, was balding, easygoing — and smitten with the pretty woman. By this time Marie had selected an alias, and was calling herself Robbi Hannon. She had also fabricated a story about being a widow who had lost her rich Texas husband to a heart attack and her young children in a car crash. Their romance blossomed and Robbi soon moved in with her sweetheart.

But the boat-building business wasn't running as smoothly as the love affair, and in 1980 the couple pulled up stakes and journeyed north to the tiny New Hampshire village of Marlow. They settled in a bungalow in the woods. John got a job as a tool-and-die-maker in the nearby town of Keene, and Robbi went to work at the Central Screw Company in the same town.

In May 1981, they were married, with the bride trimming ten years off her age and listing herself as only thirty-six.

A few months after her marriage, Robbi told John that her late husband's brother had died in Houston, Texas. She said she had to fly there to settle her former husband's estate, which was worth millions. While there, she said, she planned to visit her twin sister, Teri.

In Houston, Robbi quickly found another job as a secretary, and told her new friends and fellow employees that she was a widow expecting a multi-million dollar inheritance. Then she started complaining of illness, quit her job, flew to Dallas for a brief stay, and finally back to the comfort and safety of life with her husband in New Hampshire.

Soon, however, Robbi again began to complain of illness. She had agonizing headaches, and began to be bothered by inexplicable losses of memory. Eventually she confided to John and to her employers that she had a terminal blood disease. Her only hope of successful treatment, she said, was a doctor in Germany.

Rejecting John's pleas to accompany her, she again headed for Texas, explaining that she wanted to visit with her twin sister before flying to Germany in a last-ditch effort to find a cure for her ailment.

She flew to Dallas, but stayed only briefly before leaving for Pompano Beach, Florida, where she again found work as a secretary. This time she assumed the name of the fictional twin, Teri Martin. To complete her transformation she trimmed thirty pounds from her weight, cut her hair short, and dyed it blonde. By November 9, she was back in Dallas, and telephoned John posing as Teri, to give him the bad news — his wife, Robbi, had died.

John was grief-stricken, but his sister-in-law was a pillar of strength. Teri explained that in accordance with Robbi's wishes, she had donated her twin's body for medical research. Teri assured him that she would take care of Robbi's remaining business affairs in Texas, and that there was no reason for him to come to Dallas.

A few days later Robbi's pretty twin showed up in New Hampshire. Despite the slimmer body, the different hairstyle, and other little differences in her likes and dislikes such as smoking a different brand of cigarettes, Teri was remarkably like Robbi. But they were, after all, identical twins, as Teri pointed out and she told stories about how when they were teenagers, people would become confused over which girl was which. Teri moved in with John and they comforted each other, sharing their grief over their loss of Robbi.

Most of Robbi's acquaintances in Marlow learned of her tragic death through an obituary carried in the *Keene Sentinel* shortly after Teri showed up at her late sister's home. It read:

Robbi L. Homan

Robbi L. Homan, 37, of Marlow died Wednesday in Dallas, Texas, after a long illness.

She was born in Buffalo, N.Y., March 25, 1945, daughter of Hugh and Cindi Grayson, and had lived in Marlow for two years.

Mrs. Homan was formerly employed by Central Screw Co. in Keene and was a member of Sacred Heart Church in Tyler, Texas.

Survivors include her husband, John Homan of Marlow, and two sisters, Teri Martin of Dallas and Jean Ann Trevor of White Plains, N.Y.

Mrs. Homan had requested that her body be donated to the Medical Research Institute in Texas and that no funeral be held. Contributions may be made in her memory to a favorite charity.

However, not everyone in Marlow who had

known Robbi Homan was as ready as John was to accept the newcomer as his late wife's twin. The skeptics were especially prevalent among Robbi's former co-workers at the Central Screw Company after John and Teri stopped at the office one day. After the couple left, some people laughed about the obvious masquerade.

Robbi's former boss, Ron Oja, was one of those who was struck by Teri's remarkable similarity to her late sister, but he allowed himself to be convinced by the twin story, and Audrey Marie Hilley, *née* Robbi Homan, *née* Teri Martin, was good at convincing people of just about anything.

Nevertheless, rumors about the petite blonde were soon crackling like lightning through the normally quiet communities of Marlow and Keene. There were people who thought it was strange the way Teri had moved in with the widower and taken over her allegedly dead twin's life, even to the point of wearing Robbi's clothes. When Teri found herself a job as a secretary with a bookbinding company just over the state line in Brattleboro, Vermont, some wondered that Teri had even sought out the same kind of work as her twin.

Eyebrows were also raised over the way Robbi had left town so suddenly, not once, but twice, then mysteriously died. And it just didn't seem right that the body had been so rapidly disposed of, without her husband even going to Texas. There had been no funeral at all, in fact, even though Robbi had been a church-going woman and presumably would have wished a clergyman to give her a proper Christian send-off. It was all so very, very strange.

A few people admitted outright to their neighbors that no matter what John Homan might think, they believed Robbi had never died, and that she and Teri were the same woman. And that supposition led to another that perhaps was the most titillating of all.

Could it be, the speculation went, that the mystery woman known alternately as Robbi Homan and Teri Martin, was in fact a totally different individual — Carol Manning, a federal fugitive wanted by the FBI?

Meanwhile, as the local whispering continued to build, Marie was busily creating a brand new life history for herself as Teri, just as she had done when she was posing as Robbi. She explained that she had been living in Denver where she had been married to a military officer with whom she didn't get along. She had, therefore, no serious regrets about leaving him for Texas to care for her ailing sister, and after Robbi's tragic death, had moved on to New Hampshire, hoping to get a fresh start in life.

At last, however, Marie's phenomenal luck began to run out and no amount of personal charisma, support from trusting family and friends, or ready lies could stave off disaster.

Her former boss, Ron Oja, was sick and tired of all the scuttlebutt circulating about the twin. He decided to do a little amateur detective work and settle the matter once and for all.

He got in touch with a contact in Dallas and

asked him to check out as much information as he could from Robbi's obituary. The Dallas contact couldn't confirm a single fact. Seriously troubled by this development, Oja took his story and newfound suspicions to the Keene police.

But even the police couldn't figure out who the woman really was. And they were as unsuccessful in efforts to turn up traces of her sisters, Jean Ann Trevor and Teri Martin, as they were in locating anyone who had known Robbi Homan before she met John and appeared in New Hampshire. However, the police started getting some ideas, and one of the most disturbing possibilities led them to speculate that the woman might indeed be the federal fugitive, Carol Manning.

Carol Manning and a companion, Raymond Luc Lavasseur, were political radicals and reputed members of vicious left-wing groups known as the United Freedom Front and the Sam Melville-Jonathan Jackson Unit. Various members of the terrorist organizations were accused by federal and local authorities of involvement in a string of bank robberies, bombings and the murder of a New Jersey State Trooper.

The massive search for Mrs. Manning and Lavasseur had recently focused on the Brattleboro area after lawmen discovered a safe house they were believed to have vacated only a short time before in southeastern Vermont.

Observation of the mystery woman soon convinced police that she was not Carol Manning, but, in view of the false obituary and apparently false identities she had manufactured for herself, there seemed to be little doubt that she was running from something. And investigators came up with another federal fugitive who was known for using the alias, Teri Martin.

The fugitive the FBI was seeking was wanted on charges of violating federal drug laws. She was about the same height and weight as the local woman the New Hampshire police were watching, and she even had blonde hair.

Early in January, an FBI agent and two state policemen, one from Vermont and one from New Hampshire, stopped Marie (posing as Teri) in the parking lot of the bookbinding company as she left work, and took her to the Brattleboro Police station for questioning.

They barely got settled before the petite blonde woman blurted out a surprising story. She was none of the women she had represented herself to be, or that law enforcement authorities had speculated she might be. But she was a fugitive, she admitted, from charges pending against her in Alabama.

The police officers were stunned, but Marie seemed relieved. She said she was tired of running, and soon she was recounting the entire story of her incredible double masquerade and elaborate hoax.

John Homan was devastated by the news. There was no way that he would accept the idea that his wife was suspected of poisoning members of her own family back in Alabama.

Marie waived extradition and was returned to Alabama to face a murder charge for Frank's death, and a charge of attempted murder in the poisoning of Carol. The bad check charges were also still pending.

Marie's trials for the poisoning of her husband and daughter were held at the Calhoun County Courthouse in Anniston to packed crowds who lined up hours ahead of time to obtain seats and a chance to see the woman whom many were referring to as Arsenic Audrey. Many people brought their lunches, so they wouldn't lose their seats during the noon recesses.

The trial promised to be better than any television soap opera, and it was. Poisonings, dual identities, sex, a three-year manhunt, and eventual capture that was the next thing to accidental and may not have occurred at all had Marie not elected to kill off one of her other selves; it was stranger-than-fiction truth, and it involved one of Anniston's own.

Midway in the proceedings, a prisoner who had recently been locked up with Marie, stunned the courtroom assemblage when she testified that her former cellmate had hatched a bold and daring escape plot during the six-month pre-trial wait in the county jail. The witness said she refused to go along with the escape attempt, and Marie apparently abandoned the scheme. There seemed to be no end to Marie's surprises.

But once the true story of her coldly calculated crimes and elaborate deceptions had been unravelled and exposed in the courtroom, there was nothing left in Marie's bag of tricks that could prevent the jury of ten men and two women from returning guilty verdicts.

The next day, presiding Circuit Court Judge Sam Monk sentenced Marie to life in prison for the first-degree murder of Frank Hilley, and pronounced a sentence of twenty-years imprisonment for the poisoning of Carol. The sentences were ordered to run consecutively.

At the time Frank died, Alabama had no death penalty. Judge Monk, therefore, pronounced the maximum terms on both charges, and the earliest Marie would be eligible for parole would be 1990.

Incredibly, even after Marie's conviction and sentencing, her ability to produce bizarre surprises hadn't run its course.

Marie was sent to Alabama's Tutwiler Prison for Women near the town of Wetumpka, where she became a model prisoner and agreed to plead guilty to the remaining bad-check charges. Judge Monk tacked another year-and-a-day to her previous sentences, with the stipulation that the time was to be served concurrently with the longer terms.

It wasn't long before Marie's exemplary behavior earned her a transfer to the prison's honor dormitory, and despite her record for running and the seriousness of the crimes she was convicted of, she was given the privilege of wearing civilian clothes and occasionally dining or shopping outside the prison walls.

On some of these trips, or passes, as they are referred to by prison authorities, Marie spent time with John Homan, who had followed her to Anniston where he obtained a foundry job, and continued to give her his loyal and loving support.

She had been with John at his rented apartment in an Anniston hotel in February, 1987, on her first extended three-day pass, when she dropped from sight.

On a Sunday, the day she was to have returned to Tutwiler, Marie reportedly told her husband that she wanted to meet a friend and visit her mother's grave. She didn't want John to go with her, she claimed, because she was afraid someone might recognize them if they were together. After her visit to the cemetery, she was supposed to meet him at a restaurant — but she never showed up.

Instead, Marie left behind a farewell note advising him that she was going to Atlanta and then to Canada to start a new life. She said she hoped John would "understand and forgive" her for leaving.

Prison spokesman John Hale explained to the press: "She did not want to go back to prison. She wanted to be given a chance to get her life started over."

Law enforcement authorities in Calhoun county weren't at all surprised, and townspeople in Anniston began predicting that the fifty-three-year-old fugitive might never be captured again. Marie had learned a lot about deception and life on the run the first time she fled, and it seemed unlikely she would make the same mistakes twice.

Even as Hale release a photograph of Marie

to the press, he cautioned that she had probably changed her appearance. He quoted the prison warden and others familiar with her case with describing her as "an expert in disguising herself...changing her hair style, color, dress."

"But they all say she will always appear as a top-flight professional — a quiet, reserved member of the upper middle-class society."

Local, state and federal authorities launched another massive search for Marie. She was believed to have no more than thirty dollars with her, no credit cards and no car. Yet police warned that she was a "wily, resourceful and manipulative master criminal," and the search quickly spread throughout the nation.

Meanwhile, Prison Commissioner Morris Thigpen, who had been on the job in Alabama only three weeks, called for a review of the furlough program, while local, state and federal law enforcement agencies launched another massive search for the arsenic killer. Assistant District Attorney Joe Hubbard, who helped prosecute Marie, was outraged at her escape. "I think this is not just insane," he complained, "it's gross negligence."

Five days after Marie walked out of the prison on what was her first three-day furlough, she came up with one final, grim surprise. A woman found the gaunt body of the fugitive sprawled on the porch of a rural home less than a mile from her birthplace in Blue Mountain. She was mumbling incoherently and was covered with mud. Minutes after an ambulance arrived, she suffered a convulsion and lost consciousness. Marie died three-and-a-half hours later at the Northeast Alabama Regional Medical Center in Anniston after suffering a cardiac arrest. A doctor at the hospital had recognized her from a newspaper photograph.

Calhoun County Coroner Ralph Phillips listed hypothermia, the extreme loss of body heat, as the official cause of death.

She had apparently been crawling around in the woods, drenched by four days of intermittent cold rain in temperatures dropping to the low 30s, Phillips said.

District Attorney Robert Field was as nonplussed as anyone by the sudden, unexpected end of Anniston's notorious poisoner.

"It's unbelievable. This goes against everything she's done in the past," he told the press. "The biggest escape artist in this area in ten years, and what does she do? She ended up crawling around in the woods."

Loretta Stonebraker, who planned that hogs would eat her murdered husband's body, is led from the Parke County Courthouse.

(Photo courtesy of Torch Newspapers)

The bruising mud wrestler, "Big Helen" Williams, who helped Loretta kill her husband, is shown with her deputy at her arraignment.

(Photo courtesy of Torch Newspapers)

Michael Keen, the successful Fort Lauderdale businessman, who pushed his pregnant wife off his boat and watched her drown.

(Miami Herald photo by Walter Michot)

The pretty and innocent-looking housewife and mother, Patricia Prewitt, who put a bullet through her sleeping husband's skull.

(Photo courtesy of Holden Progress)

British heir to a title and fortune, Michael Telling, pictured on his wedding day with his American bride, Monika Zumsteg-Telling, his victim in a grisly murder.

(A/P WIDE WORLD PHOTOS)

Marie Hilley, a notorious poisoner, eluded her captors for 4 years in one of the most bizarre masquerades in the history of American crime. (Photo courtesy of Eddie Motes)

Marie Hilley as she is returned from New Hampshire to Alabama to face murder charges.

(Photo courtesy of Eddie Motes)

Reverend Grady Young (handcuffed) as he is escorted from Memorial Services for his murdered wife.

(Photo courtesy of Tom Thompson and Peninsula Daily News)

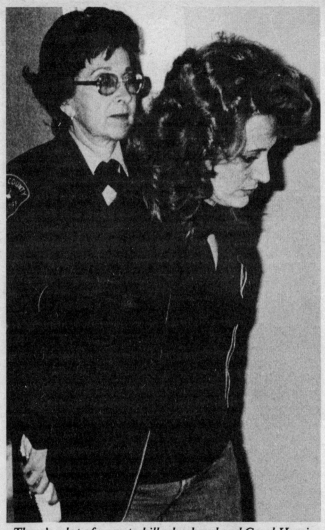

There's a lot of ways to kill a husband and Carol Hargis, right, tried most of them before she finally succeeded.

(Photo courtesy of Union-Tribune Publishing Co.)

Katie Harper (in handcuffs, above left) and Sandy Harper (in handcuffs, below right) as they are being led out of Court of Queen's Bench in Winnipeg during Canada's longest-running murder case.

(Courtesy Gerard Kwiatkowski and Winnipeg Sun)

Chiropractor James B. Klindt is escorted from his office by police after his arrest for a murder which would involve crime experts in a grim puzzle.

CHAPTER SIX

DEATH FOR THE PERFECT PREACHER'S WIFE

It was 5:48 P.M. on a quiet Saturday afternoon when dispatcher Ruth Bemis took a call on the 911 emergency number at the Port Angeles, Washington, Police Department.

A man who identified himself as the Reverend Grady Young reported that his wife appeared to have been shot, and that she was unconscious and did not seem to be breathing.

Mrs. Young was lying on the porch of their mobile home, which was the parsonage for the Hillcrest Baptist Church on Black Diamond Road, the minister said.

The church and parsonage were just outside the city limits of the isolated papermill and logging town along the south shore of the Juan de Fuca Strait in Washington State. The

119

dispatcher quickly relayed the call to the Clallam County Sheriff's Department. She said there was an apparent death at the parsonage — and that the aid unit probably wasn't necessary.

When Sheriff's Deputy Michael Hopf arrived at the parsonage minutes later, he found a matronly woman who appeared to be in her mid-fifties sprawled facedown on the steps of the trailer's back porch. A couple of video-cassette tapes were scattered on the ground a few feet from the body.

Hopf checked for life signs and was unable to detect a pulse. The body was cold. There was a small blood spot on her back, and a smear of blood on her face.

A slight, bespectacled, balding man in a dark suit was leaning against the right front fender of a car as officers and an emergency aid unit from Dry Creek arrived. He identified himself as the Reverend Grady Young, the woman's husband, and said he thought his wife, Elva Mae, had been shot.

A closer examination of the body by Sheriff's Sergeant Jim Newton disclosed matted blood on the woman's head, and holes in the front and back of her blouse. A few inches away, the officer discovered a battered particle of lead which he recognized as the slug from a bullet. There was no gun in sight.

The clergyman told investigators that his wife had left early that afternoon to shop for groceries and keep a 2 P.M. hairdressing appointment. He had also left for Port Angeles to buy a styptic pencil for shaving cuts, Young said, and when he returned a short time later he found his wife's body on the back porch of their trailer home. Hesitating only long enough to check for a pulse and to determine that he couldn't help her, he had hurried to the church and dialed the police emergency number.

The sixty-year-old minister was surprisingly calm, but some of the investigators assumed that his profession had prepared him to keep his emotions under control in the face of sudden tragedy.

As deputies began sealing off the investigation area with red ribbon, other officers were focusing their attention on a side window of the parsonage. A garbage can had been placed underneath the dining room window and the screen and a screwdriver were found lying nearby.

It appeared that Mrs. Young had surprised a burglar inside the trailer when she returned from shopping, and as she turned to flee back outside she had been shot to death by the startled intruder. Grocery bags filled with meat, vegetables and ice cream that was already beginning to melt were still stacked inside the trunk of her parked car. A receipt inside one of the bags indicated that Mrs. Young had moved through the checkout counter at a local supermarket at 4:24 P.M.

A car carrying a church deacon, Peter Hof, and his wife, Juanita, who owned the parsonage, pulled to a stop at the church as investigators were arriving, and the couple ran to the mobile home. Mrs. Hof leaned over the body and picked up her friend's limp hand and then, assured that the woman was beyond help, gently placed it back down on the porch.

Ignoring her own distress, Mrs. Hof approached the minister and asked if she could help him by notifying his five children of the tragedy.

"No, not now. I want to see how this turns out," he replied.

As the body of his dead wife lay only a few feet away, his second remark seemed as strange as his first: "I hope the church has a meeting tomorrow, and lets me know whether they want to retain me as pastor."

Major Fred DeFrang of the Clallam County Sheriff's Department took charge at the investigation scene and called for search dogs to be brought to the parsonage. As the crime was fresh, there seemed to be an excellent chance they could pick up the killer's tracks.

When the bloodhounds arrived, their handler led them to the garbage can. Almost immediately they picked up a scent and headed off through the surrounding woods, down a steep ravine and on to a street leading toward the center of Port Angeles. There, however, they lost the trail and were unable to pick it up again. Later that evening and the next day they picked up scents several times, but the trails usually led no farther than the nearby mailbox or the church. Eventually, more than two dozen officers, with the tracking dogs, searched a two-mile area surrounding the church and parsonage.

After the body of Mrs. Young was removed, her husband was asked to accompany a deputy on a walk through the trailer to check for missing possessions. It was already early evening and the trees at the edge of the clearing were beginning to blur into indistinct shadows when the men entered the parsonage.

A note from Reverend Young to his wife indicating he would be home at 5:45 P.M., was on the kitchen counter. Throughout their marriage, he had been considerate about keeping her informed of his whereabouts and plans, and he was known by family members and friends for his loving habit of leaving notes for her.

The trailer walls were decorated with children's small drawings and notices and reminders were stuck to the refrigerator door. A woman's pink robe hung listlessly from a hanger in the bathroom — and empty .22-caliber rifle cartridge casings were scattered on the floor of the kitchen and dining room, as well as on the back porch near the body. There were additional indications that the modest, neatly kept parson's home had been violated by an intruder.

Quietly and still without any seeming emotion, Young began counting off a list of belongings he said were missing. A .35-millimeter camera and flash attachment, two pairs of binoculars, a jewelry box and about five hundred to six hundred dollars worth of jewelry, a brown briefcase, a 12-gauge double-barreled shotgun and a semi-automatic .22-caliber Marlin rifle were among the items that Young reported as having apparently been taken. He said he also owned a .38-caliber revolver which had been given to him by his father.

He explained that he had never fired the old shotgun, which was also his father's, and had only recently purchased the target rifle in Seattle, because he was thinking of going deer hunting and wanted to practice his marksmanship. He had ammunition for the rifle in the house, but neither of the weapons were kept loaded.

Whoever had hurriedly ransacked the parsonage had left behind several articles, such as an expensive coin collection and gleaming portable radio that were openly visible and more valuable than some of the missing pieces. The listed articles were typical of those a child or teenager might take, investigators realized. The presence of the garbage can pulled under the window also seemed to point to an amateurish young burglar — the kind of thief who, startled and frightened, might have panicked when he was suddenly confronted by Mrs. Young, and shot her.

Another possible suspect surfaced when police were notified by church members that they had seen a suspicious-looking man carrying a pillowcase filled with something. Police circulated an artist's drawing of the man, and noted that he was wanted for questioning.

Reverend Young stayed overnight with a church deacon from his congregation while investigators kept the trailer roped off, under guard, and continued their efforts to piece together the last hours and minutes of the victim's life.

They had learned that early on the afternoon of Mrs. Young's death, Peter Hof had shown up and cut some brush that was encroaching upon the trailer home. She had seemed to be in good spirits and was eagerly looking forward to the impending visit of a daughter and a grandchild.

After both Mrs. Young and the deacon left, according to her husband, Reverend Young cleaned up and changed his clothes. Then he scribbled the note, checked to see that the bedroom and dining room windows were partly open, and left for town.

Reverend Young said he drove first to a park, then to a scenic area called Ediz Hook, which juts into the Juan de Fuca Strait just east of the town, to relax before shopping at a couple of stores, buying the styptic pencil and returning home. He parked his pickup truck at the church, and was walking to the parsonage when he saw his wife's body, he said.

The minister explained that he went to the church to call for help instead of using the phone inside the trailer because he didn't want to disturb anything that might be helpful in the investigation.

The day after Elva Mae's murder, when television and newspaper reporters asked the minister about his reaction to finding his wife dead, he replied that he was, "in kind of a state of shock, but I prayed as best I could. I prayed mainly for my family, for the Lord comforting and underpinning them in the crisis that had arisen."

His wife was already dead, he said. "We don't pray for people who are dead; we pray for people who are alive."

One of the most highly respected forensic pathologists in the Pacific Northwest was flown to Port Angeles from Portland, Oregon, to head the autopsy examination on Mrs. Young. Dr. William Brady, who was Oregon State Medical Examiner before he went into private practice as a forensic pathologist, inspected the body and determined that the victim was struck by three bullets.

According to his report and later courtroom testimony, one of the shots was apparently deflected by her purse and a videocassette she was carrying, causing the bullet to tumble and strike her sideways in the chest. It failed to penetrate the skin. Another lethal shot crashed into her back, passed through her spine and struck her heart.

A third shot, which appeared to have been the last triggered, and which had been fired execution style at extremely close range, entered her head behind her left ear. The slug split inside the cranium and one piece of it passed diagonally through her brain before lodging in the right side of her head.

A spent bullet, apparently the first one fired and the one that struck Mrs. Young's purse, was found on the porch by investigators.

Authorities dropped the man with the pillow-case as a potential suspect, after he walked into the Sheriff's Department, identified himself, and was questioned and cleared. But there was yet another suspect because when a married woman is murdered, her husband is almost always one of the first people to be investigated — even if he is a clergyman.

However, the Reverend Young was about as unlikely a killer as police anywhere could produce. According to everything investigators could learn from friends, parishioners and neighbors, the Youngs had enjoyed a long, fruitful and happy marriage with no history of discord.

There seemed no hint as well that throughout their thirty-eight year marriage, the Reverend Young had strayed into other pastures and had a fling with another woman. He had no history of mental illness, and his wife had not been heavily insured. There simply seemed to be no motive for the respected clergyman to have murdered his wife.

And Elva Mae, friends insisted, had been the perfect preacher's wife.

The Reverend Young had also been a thoughtful and caring husband and father, as well as a devoted spiritual leader to his flock. He kept Mondays as special days for he and his wife to enjoy together, and they often took advantage of the picturesque North Olympic Peninsula by taking long nature walks or hikes.

When he returned from work each day, the

first thing he did was find Elva Mae — who was usually in the kitchen preparing supper — and give her a big hug and a kiss.

Although to outsiders he could appear to be a stern and unemotional man who ran his home according to the scriptures, those who knew him best insisted that he was fair and loving and tried to keep up with society's rapidly changing mores in his relationships with his family.

The couple had met while Elva Mae was still attending high school in Tahoka, Texas, and married in June 1948, a few weeks after her graduation. They both attended Corpus Christi University, then moved to Fort Worth, Texas, where Grady completed his seminary training, before they relocated to the Northwest and he began his ministry.

They served at several small churches, including pastorates at Leavenworth, and Everett, Washington and Madras, Oregon before moving to Port Angeles. Immediately before moving to Port Angeles in 1983, the couple lived in Washington's state capital, Olympia. Grady worked there for twenty-five years as a case work supervisor for the State Department of Social and Health Services. He was used to working at outside jobs in addition to his church duties in order to support his family and help his children through college.

Elva Mae took a job as a seamstress with an upholstering business while the family was living in Olympia. She had obtained more than enough experience for the job while sewing for herself and her three daughters.

As the couple moved themselves and their children from community to community, Elva Mae always took an active part in church affairs, dutifully playing the piano at services, teaching Sunday School and assisting with youth activities.

In Port Angeles she also served as director of the Retired Senior Volunteer Program, which served a two-county area, and was senior nutrition director at a nursing home. Her life had been filled with activity and love.

Just as her husband was a good and caring father, she was a good and affectionate mother. And she was a devoted homemaker who enjoyed baking bread and pastries for her family. When her two sons and her daughters were growing up, Elva Mae sometimes invited their sweethearts to join the family at meals for delicious southern-style chicken dinners. And she sat up nights with her daughters after they returned home from dates or school and church activities, laughing and giggling just as if she herself was one of the teenagers.

Now that happy life was over and her widower and their children forlornly gathered in the chapel of a Port Angeles funeral home, Reverend Young observed that life would be difficult without his wife's company, and her devoted support for his ministry. And, true to his calling, the clergyman indicated he had already ruled out any desire for revenge against the killer of his loyal spouse.

"My faith has sustained me this far and I feel it will continue," he told a reporter for the Port Angeles *Daily News*.

"To me, revenge means something that it doesn't to some people. To me, it means personal retribution. I don't see there's any place for that."

Law enforcement officers investigating the brutal murder of the gentle woman shot at the entrance of her own home weren't after revenge either, but they were determined to see justice done.

While looking around the Young home, Detective Don Kirst pushed aside some cardboard boxes under the clergyman's bed and uncovered a brown briefcase containing a pair of binoculars. Aware that Young had reported two sets of binoculars missing from the parsonage, Kirst wondered to himself: "How many binoculars does this guy own?" Then he found another pair of binoculars, a box of .22 caliber ammunition, and a camera and flash attachment. And in the minister's study, the detective found a pair of rubber surgical gloves stuffed behind files in the top drawer. Police technicians had already turned up in the house fingerprints that appeared to have been made with rubber gloves.

Detective Nick Turner made the next major discovery when he opened two suitcases taken from one of the clergyman's closets. Elva Mae's missing cream-colored plastic jewelry case was tucked inside one of them.

Then Deputy Matt Dalton opened the doors to the crawl space under the mobile home, and pulled out a plastic bag. Inside the bag were a .22-caliber rifle and a disassembled shotgun with the pieces held together by masking tape.

The personal property that Reverend Young had reported missing from his home had been found, and investigators now had a pretty good idea *who* had killed Elva Mae. But they hadn't yet figured out *why*.

Three nights after Elva Mae's murder, and a few hours after the missing property was picked up by deputies, inspected, photographed and logged as evidence, Clallam County Sheriff's Sergeant Bill Henry had another talk with Reverend Young.

After warning the preacher about his rights against self-incrimination, Henry asked him to describe, item by item, the property reported missing. Reverend Young complied. Then the officer asked if there was anything else he wanted to talk about. Calm as could be, the poker-faced preacher said there wasn't.

Sergeant Henry told the clergyman that he believed there had never been a burglary and that Reverend Young himself had shot his wife. Still, the minister appeared unshaken.

Even when Henry reached into his desk drawer and pulled out photographs of the items reported stolen that had been recovered from inside and under the house, the minister remained unflappable. But he did concede that the briefcase, binoculars, camera, shotgun and rifle in the photos looked like his property.

Henry arrested Reverend Young on suspicion of murdering his wife, and had him booked in the Clallam County Jail.

Shock crackled through the community like a lightning flash. With a county population of under forty thousand, Port Angeles is a small town, friendly and concerned about its sons and daughters and until Mrs. Young was killed, there hadn't been a known murder committed there for years.

The congregation of Hillcrest Baptist Church was especially hard hit by what was shaping up to be a double tragedy. Could it be, some wondered, that the man who had stood in the pulpit and preached the gospel to them for the past three years was a hypocrite who had not only sinned but broken the Sixth Commandment, "Thou Shalt Not Kill"?

Many of Reverend Young's parishioners found it difficult to believe the terrible accusations lodged against such a good man, an excellent preacher who was concerned about his flock. One young couple who were baptized by him recalled that when their son had been burned severely, the preacher visited with the child for fourteen consecutive days at the hospital. Deacon Hof was quoted in the press as sadly conceding, "We're all hurt by this. They were a very loving couple, just hard to beat. It's unbelievable."

The day after his arrest, the clergyman was

formally charged in Clallam County Superior Court with first-degree murder, and bail was set at $75,000. County Prosecutor David Bruneau said he believed the slaying was premeditated.

Court documents filed by Bruneau indicated that discovery of the items Young had reported stolen led investigators to conclude that "what appeared to be a burglary more likely was a scene made to appear like a burglary."

Even though $75,000 was relatively low for a first-degree murder charge, Young was unable to immediately post bail, and later that day, sheriff's deputies escorted the handcuffed clergyman from the Clallam County Jail in Port Angeles to the Hillcrest Baptist Church, where memorial services were scheduled for his wife. He was permitted to exchange his baggy orange jail jumpsuit for a dark blue business suit, and moments before the services began, he entered the chapel.

The tiny church, which despite Reverend Young's tireless efforts to recruit newcomers to the congregation, had seldom attracted more than thirty-five people for services, was filled with more than two hundred people. So many people crowded inside that some mourners had to stand in the aisles, and one parishioner helping to direct traffic to parking spaces outside told a reporter, "Grady always wanted a turnout like this."

Reverend Young's handcuffs were removed just before he walked from the sanctuary. Flanked by two burly sheriff's deputies, the frail suspect sat silently and without obvious emotion in a front pew a few feet from his children, while a retired minister — one of four clergymen, all friends of the Youngs', who eulogized the dead woman — compared her to the famous Biblical women, Hannah, Abigail, Ruth and Deborah. "She had experience with God," the preacher told the hushed gathering, "and she believed the promise of God. She called her household to God."

Elva Mae's favorite hymn, "O Perfect Love," was played on the church organ by her longtime friend, Mrs. Hof.

Reverend Young stood during the hymns but did not sing. During the final prayer, five minutes before the simple hour-long service ended, he nodded to the deputies guarding him and they escorted him from the church. The handcuffs were replaced on his wrists for the drive back to the jail.

Reverend Young pleaded innocent at his arraignment, and bail was lowered to a $5,000 cash bond, which his children provided. "We believe our father is innocent," Air Force Captain Phillip Young, one of the couple's children, told the judge. "We loved our mother and we love our father very dearly."

While his defense was being prepared for the trial, Reverend Young was released into the custody of his retired minister friend. His movements were initially restricted to Clallam County, but the terms of his release were later modified by the court and he was permitted to travel to Seattle, Oklahoma and Texas for holidays and to visit family members.

Three hours before the minister was released from the jail, some twenty-five members of his church had filed out of the chapel following Sunday services. At that service, the Reverend Weldon Stevens advised the tiny congregation to look to the Bible for strength and guidance in their time of need. And he urged that they not rush to a judgement of their pastor, but instead, treat him as a wounded Christian brother who needed their support.

"Someone once said that the Christian army is the only army in the world that shoots its wounded," he declared. "That's not what the Bible tells us to do."

Reverend Stevens said he supported his fellow minister and would continue to do so. "He's innocent," Stevens reminded the congregation, "until proven guilty."

No action was taken either by the congregation, or by the Olympic Baptist Association, to remove Reverend Young from his position as church pastor or from the ministry. Much later, Reverend Cecil Sims, executive director of the Northwest Baptist Convention, explained from his office in Portland, Oregon to an inquiring journalist that "it is not the prerogative of the denomination to withdraw ordination papers." Reverend Young's ministry, he said, would have to stand on its own merits.

Just after Thanksgiving, however, Reverend Young resigned as pastor of the Hillcrest Baptist Church. A short time later he accepted an invitation to teach a Bible studies class to young men at a church he was attending in the town of Sequim, a few miles east of Port Angeles.

Meanwhile, the accused wife-slayer's attorney, Craig Ritchie, was labeling the prosecution's charges against Reverend Young as "the case of the missing motive."

"The first thing a thinking person would ask is, 'Why'd he do it?'" the attorney was quoted in the press.

It was still a good question, but by the time Prosecutor David Bruneau took his case before a Clallam County Superior Court jury of four men and eight women in January 1987, he had decided that the defendant had a quixotically simple motive. He was merely tired of being married. Anxious to avoid losing his job and ending his career amid the scandal of divorce, he waited in ambush for his wife to return from her shopping trip, and coldly shot her to death. Then, the prosecutor told the jury, Reverend Young staged a phony burglary at the parsonage as a cover-up.

Bruneau said Reverend Young intended to commit the perfect crime. After the clergyman had bought the rifle in Seattle, declared Bruneau: "All he had to do was wait until no one else was around to kill his wife."

The prosecutor said that as Mrs. Young entered the parsonage, her husband shot her in the chest. As she turned to flee, he shot her in the back, then while she was lying on the porch, her husband fired the final shot into her head.

Addressing the jury in Reverend Young's defense, Ritchie, a former county prosecutor, maintained that the early indications of a solution to the mystery were correct: Mrs. Young had been shot by a burglar she surprised.

He also told the jury they would hear testimony that a suspicious person was seen in the area before Mrs. Young was shot, and that the husband of one of the members of the church's congregation believed he had been ordered by God to kill his wife.

And two different teams of tracking dogs on two different days, he said, followed a scent from the parsonage into the valley — one time running past the defendant.

An FBI expert testified that the bullet that struck Mrs. Young in the back was fired from the .22-caliber rifle found under the parsonage. The bullet fragment found in Mrs. Young's brain, however, could not be positively identified as being fired from the same weapon.

Crime laboratory technicians also identified Reverend Young's fingerprints and palm prints on the plastic bag wrapped around the rifle.

Dr. Brady, the forensic pathologist flown in from Portland to perform the autopsy, testified that the head wound resembled those seen in professional murders. He remarked that in his previous experience as a pathologist in New York City, he had seen similar injuries to "a large number of young men recovered from the Hudson River with bullet wounds in the back of their heads." Asked by Bruneau if Mrs. Young's head wound was "an execution-style wound," he indicated that it was.

Some of the most unexpected, distressing and controversial testimony at the trial came from Dr. Brady, who reported that his examination of the victim indicated the presence of an alcoholic liver ailment. He observed that individual tolerance to alcohol varies, especially in women, but remarked, "Ordinarily I would say this is a pretty heavy boozer."

The doctor conceded that other conditions could cause similar fat deposits in the liver, but said there was no evidence she suffered from any of those ailments.

This surprising disclosure was just one more shock to the family and friends of the Youngs. They were quick to object, both among themselves and to newsmen, and when called as witnesses by Ritchie. Eventually, more than thirty witnesses who were friends, relatives or acquaintances of the victim testified that they had never known her to drink alcoholic beverages. Witnesses insisted that she was strongly opposed to booze. The Reverend Fred Jewell, the first pastor of the Hillcrest Baptist Church, who retired in 1973 but returned to his former pulpit on an interim basis after the shooting, stated: "I don't think Elva Mae Young ever took a drink in her life." And a Port Angeles doctor testified that he had prescribed medications for Elva Mae that could have caused the damage that led the pathologist to conclude she had a drinker's liver.

The Reverend Young's own moral fiber was questioned when the prosecution called to the stand an attractive twenty-eight-year-old woman with whom he had spent considerable time, counseling about marital problems and religious concerns. The minister had talked with the woman at her home, by telephone, and drove her, along with one of her daughters and her mother, to Seattle, where he purchased the .22 caliber rifle about three weeks before his wife's slaying.

The woman, who was the mother of three girls, denied that there had been any romantic link between her and the preacher, and said the only time they were ever alone was for a brief period at the church shortly before the Seattle trip.

Reverend Young's defense attorney labored during the trial to show that Elva Mae could indeed have been shot after surprising a burglar. He worked hard to convince the jury that there was no true motive for the clergyman to have murdered the loving wife who had stood by him so loyally for nearly forty years.

And he suggested that there were others with more believable motives who might have wished to harm either Reverend or Mrs. Young.

With the jury out of the courtroom, Defense Attorney Ritchie suggested that the husband of the troubled woman the minister had been counseling might have been angry at the Youngs because of their involvement with his wife and the girls during the marital difficulties. But when the jury was seated a short time later, her husband testified that the Reverend Young had in fact listened to his side of the story and helped him visit the children.

The husband, who described himself as a prophet, also talked about conversations with God, and about messages from bees.

A few days before the end of the trial, someone telephoned the Clallam County Sheriff's Department and announced that a man claimed Elva Mae was shot after he drove a truck to the Young home and waited outside as a lookout while two companions burglarized the parsonage.

The information was relayed to Ritchie, and a sworn statement was provided by a man who quoted a relative as saying that the Youngs surprised the burglars inside the parsonage. The reputed lookout was said to have related that one of the burglars claimed he pushed Elva Mae out of the way to escape, and that the preacher fired a gun at him but hit her, instead, according to the statement.

When Ritchie asked to delay the trial to further investigate the statement, his motion was denied by Clallam County Superior Court Judge Gary W. Velie. The judge observed that the defense attorney had had the previous weekend in which to corroborate the deposition. The two individuals identified in the deposition were in jail awaiting trials on unrelated criminal charges.

Judge Velie ruled in chambers that the jury would not be permitted to hear testimony about the reputed break-in because the information could not be corroborated by the reputed burglars, and consequently, it was hearsay.

Major DeFrang was quoted in a news account as explaining the sheriff's department did not further investigate the story because it wasn't credible. "There's no crime here to investigate. This is just unrelated fabrication by non-credible providers," he declared.

Major DeFrang also noted that, among other calls received by the sheriff's department about the case, was a tip from a psychic who claimed that Reverend Young's defense attorney shot Elva Mae.

Shortly before summations, Reverend Young took the stand in his own defense. Asked by Ritchie if he had killed his wife, he responded with a one-word reply: "No."

The jury decided otherwise! After twelve-and-one-half hours of deliberation that took place over two days, the panel returned a unanimous verdict of guilty to first-degree murder. Washington State has no death penalty so the maximum sentence available to Judge Velie for conviction of premeditated murder was 320 months, slightly more than twenty-six-and-one-half years in prison. The minimum possible sentence was 240 months, twenty years.

Approximately one month after the verdict was reported, Reverend Young appeared before the judge for sentencing. Ritchie pleaded for the minimum sentence. But Prosecutor Bruneau asked for the maximum penalty.

Bruneau argued that the preacher ambushed his wife, "then blasted her into eternity." He described the convicted wife-killer as "a person who is full of deceit, full of treachery."

Judge Velie sentenced the sixty-one-year-old clergyman to 280 months — twenty-three-and-one-half years — in prison. He is serving the sentence at the state penitentiary at Walla Walla.

CHAPTER SEVEN

HOW MANY WAYS
CAN ONE MAN DIE?

There may have been a few eyebrows raised when handsome David Hargis tied the knot with a woman almost half again as old as he. But the tongue-wagging didn't go much further than that, because Hargis was a mature, self-assured young man who seemed well able to take good care of himself and his family.

At twenty-three, with a thirty-six-year-old wife, Carol Louise, he had long ago proven himself as a drill instructor and sergeant attached to the Marine Corps Recruit Depot at San Diego. There, he spent his days separating the men from the boys by putting recruits through their paces in classrooms, on the gunnery ranges, obstacle courses and drill fields.

But once he was home he dropped the spit

and polish, the harshly barked commands, and the abrasive competition among recruit instructors, and was content with the lighter and more relaxing lifestyle of devoted husband, and father to two little boys.

His maturity and devotion to his family was evidenced in many ways, including a $20,000 life insurance policy. He wanted to know that if anything happened to him, Carol and the boys would have more than the usual Marine Survivor Benefits to help get them off to a new start.

He was proud of the wispy little woman with the peppery temper and the sandy red hair who was his wife. And he also got along with her best friend, Natha Mary DePew.

A solidly constructed twenty-seven-year-old woman with close-cropped hair, firm, well-defined muscles, tattooed arms and a self-confident swagger, Natha Mary DePew made no serious attempt to cover up her affection for Carol. Called Terry by most of her friends, she spent a lot of time in the Hargis house, both while David was home, and while he was away.

If Terry seemed to spend just as much time with Carol as David did, it didn't appear to either worry him or make him jealous. He, himself, enjoyed the brash, tough-talking young woman's company. She was a good companion to tip a few beers with or to set off on a snake-hunting expedition into the heat-baked canyons around San Diego where western diamondback rattlers, as big around the middle as a man's clenched fist, could be found sunning themselves on boulders and rocky outcrops.

He was so sure of himself, and of those around him, that he even laughed off his sons' sixteen-year-old babysitter's warning that Carol and Terry were talking about killing him for his life insurance.

Carol and Terry, however, were dead serious!

Carol wanted the insurance money, and she offered her friend a big chunk of the windfall if she would help get rid of the young marine. Terry was agreeable, but the problem was how to go about the job.

During approximately three weeks of plotting David's death, sometimes over coffee or beer, they came up with a dozen or more ways to kill him. Some, though uniformly unsuccessful, were devilishly imaginative.

One of the most chilling schemes called for secreting a rattlesnake in the unsuspecting marine's bed. The women spent most of a day searching rugged, rocky Black's Canyon before giving up on the plan because they couldn't find a snake.

Once, as they were talking casually of murder in front of the babysitter, Carol said she was thinking of putting a tarantula in her husband's bed. She pointed out that she could always say that the fearsome spider must have escaped when the boys left the cover off its terrarium.

Carol was apparently unaware, as many people are, that although the huge hairy spiders are poisonous, their bite usually has little effect on humans or other warm-blooded animals.

The women never got around to putting the spider in David's bed. Instead they decided he could be introduced to the poison in a more novel manner. They baked him a fresh blackberry pie, and slipped a tarantula venom sac inside. That caper failed when the appreciative marine took a few nibbles, pulled the curious-looking object out, set it beside his plate, then finished the pie.

Carol and Terry weren't easily discouraged. There were still other plans to try: like injecting air into his veins while he was sleeping to create an embolism and cause a fatal heart attack. That scheme collapsed when the tip of the hypodermic syringe broke off before they could administer the injection.

Disappointed but unbowed after each failure they continued to huddle over the kitchen table, letting their malevolent imaginations soar.

They talked of whipping up a potentially lethal breakfast by dropping LSD into the French toast batter. If David hallucinated while he was driving to the base he might have a wreck, they reasoned, and with luck Carol could be a widow before nightfall. Even if they hadn't abandoned it, that manoeuvre would have been doomed to failure, because cooking destroys the chemical composition of the hallucinogenic drug.

Mixing lye into David's food was also considered for a while as a possible murder device, but for some reason or other they never tried it.

They also talked of slipping bullets into the carburetor of his truck, theorizing that when he started the vehicle he would either blow it up or shoot himself. But Carol decided against that idea; she wanted the truck to survive David's death.

Loosening the driveshaft and steering column of the truck so that it would go out of control and crash while he was driving was another suggestion they talked over and eventually discarded.

A faked accidental electrocution was another possibility. They figured they could carry it off by dropping a naked electrical cord into the shower while he was bathing.

The women also discussed running him down with his own truck or a car.

Finally, after three frustrating weeks of botched efforts and abandoned schemes, they settled on bludgeoning him to death and dumping his body in a deserted canyon or strip of desert to make it appear he was robbed and beaten by strangers.

After they settled on their new plan, Carol took a six-and-one-half-pound lead window sash weight from her garage and delivered it to Terry's apartment. It seemed to be the perfect weapon to knock out the marine sergeant. Terry put the weight behind her apartment door, where it would be handy when needed.

Based on later accounts by Terry to law

enforcement authorities, her subsequent court-room testimony, and other elements of the police investigation, on the night of July 20, 1977, David was given an open can of beer that Carol had laced heavily with tranquilizers. A short time later he was in his bedroom, deep in sleep.

According to Terry's story, she then pulled on a pair of gloves, picked up the sash weight, slipped into the bedroom and stood over the sleeping marine.

"I'm sorry, Dave," she murmured staring down at him. He looked so peaceful and defenseless that she walked out of the room.

Carol was upset, Terry claimed, and told her, "It's got to be done tonight."

Terry swallowed a couple of tranquilizers and washed them down with a beer in order to relax. It was after 2 A.M., July 21, when she padded back into the bedroom, once more whispered an apology to the sleeping man — and swung the lead weight. She smashed his head over and over again with the weight, then rushed from the bedroom.

Moments later the injured man weakly called his wife's name.

Terry said she hung her head on Carol's shoulder, sobbing.

"Don't worry," she quoted Carol as reassuring her, "everything's going to work out OK."

Terry walked back into the room and hit David again with the heavy weight. This time he stayed quiet.

The bedclothing, bed, and bedroom walls

were a mess. Even the ceiling was splattered with blood and gore from the terrible beatings. Carrying water and rags, Carol joined Terry inside the room and began to clean up.

They pressed tape over the openings of David's ears in an effort to stop some of the bleeding, and wrestled a shirt, pants and a coat onto his limp body. Then Carol helped her friend lug the victim outside and prop him up in the passenger seat of the truck. Terry drove off to get rid of the body while Carol returned to the house to continue with the cleanup. Her two young sons continued to sleep, apparently undisturbed by the ruckus.

Terry drove several miles east of San Diego to a bridge over a dry creek bed east of the small town of Ramona in the Black's Canyon area. There, in the darkness and isolation of a rocky wasteland ringed by scattered Indian reservations, she pulled the body of the marine out of the truck, and dropped it over the side of the bridge. She was climbing back into the truck when she remembered she had forgotten to pull the tape off David's ears.

When Terry returned to the apartment, Carol had finished cleaning. She had painted over the blood on the ceiling and walls. Then, with David dead, his body dumped, and the bedroom cleaned, it was time to carry out the next stage of the scheme.

Carol telephoned a San Diego County Sheriff's substation and tearfully told a deputy there that her husband was missing. She had barely begun to sob out her story when the deputy advised her he had to place her call on hold. After several minutes, the deputy finally returned to the phone and finished taking the missing persons report.

A few minutes after noon, a sheriff's department search team in a helicopter spotted a body sprawled near a bridge over the Santa Ysabel Creek in Black's Canyon. It was the missing marine drill sergeant.

Early news accounts reported that the young noncommissioned officer was found dead from multiple stab wounds. But San Diego County Coroner's authorities quickly ascertained that the victim had not been stabbed, but savagely bludgeoned. Pathologists determined he was struck repeatedly on the head and neck with a heavy, metallic object. He was apparently still alive, although probably unconscious, when dropped off the bridge.

The widow and her friend told investigators basically the same story Carol had related to sheriff's department authorities earlier that morning. They explained that David and Terry had driven to the canyon to look for snakes, but after a while they ran out of beer. So David sent Terry off to buy some while he stayed behind with a group of men they had met on the hunt. But when Terry returned, David had disappeared.

If deputies weren't already mistrustful of the yarn, they became suspicious after peeking at the truck the women said had been driven to and from the snake hunt. It sparkled from a recent wash. Whoever had washed it, however, had missed some blood inside, especially heavy stains on the back of the seat cushion on the passenger's side. The stains weren't missed by the investigators, nor was the bloodstained clothing they found in Terry's apartment.

Terry was placed under arrest and she began to talk almost immediately. The next day Carol was also picked up by police and the women were charged with murder.

A few days after the murder, a tape recording was made of a conversation Terry had with sheriff's detectives, in which she admitted that she bludgeoned the victim and dumped his body over the bridge after his wife promised her $15,000 and his truck. "It started three weeks ago. Carol told me she wanted David out of the way. She wanted his insurance money," Terry declared.

Then she detailed the bizarre schemes the two women had concocted to murder the unsuspecting marine NCO.

Carol continued to protest that she was innocent, and insisted that all the blame lay on the shoulders of her former friend, Terry DePew.

Despite her incriminating statement to detectives, Terry pleaded not guilty. Almost four months later she went on trial for murder, before Judge William T. Low, in San Diego County Superior Court.

Midway through the proceeding, after the tape recording carrying her confession was played for the jury, she interrupted the trial and advised the court that she wished to change her plea to guilty. Before accepting the plea and dismissing the jury, however, the judge asked her if the tape-recorded account of the slaying was true.

"Yes, it is," she replied in a barely audible voice. "I killed him — beat him to death," she admitted.

"For what reason did you kill him?" Judge Low asked.

"I really don't know. There was money involved, from Carol Hargis," she said.

Judge Low accepted a plea of guilty to first-degree murder. Several weeks later, with her face frozen into a sullen mask and the sleeves of her shirt rolled up to display her tattoos, the dungaree-clad defendant again stood before the judge and was sentenced to life in prison.

In pronouncing the sentence, the judge described Terry as a danger to society and characterized the beating as the "most brutal, basic way of killing. It occurred in his own house, with Mrs. Hargis' two sons in the next room," he said. "There were ten blows to the head, three to the neck. Blood was spattered all over the room."

Less than a week after Terry's trial had ended so abruptly, she was called as the state's star witness in Carol's murder trial.

Appearing more confident than at her own trial, the stocky witness stalked to the stand and once again recounted the story of the conspiracy and murder that took the life of David Hargis.

The babysitter also testified that only four days before he was reported missing, the two women had talked openly about putting a tarantula in the unsuspecting marine sergeant's bed. During Terry's abbreviated trial, the girl also recounted the conversation she had overheard between the two women.

"Carol said all she had to do was dump the body in the mountains or in the canyon by my house, and discussed all the money she'd get," the girl testified.

In light of Terry's and the babysitter's testimony, the bloodstains and other physical evidence collected by the investigative team, the odds seemed to be heavily stacked against the widow.

And even then the state had one more startling surprise up its sleeve.

Prosecutors had a tape recording of the telephone call Carol had made to the sheriff's department substation to report her husband missing. The tape, which had been left running while she was on hold and chatting with Terry as she waited for the deputy to return to the telephone, was played for the jury.

The jurors heard Carol telephone the substation and tearfully tell the deputy who answered that her husband was missing.

Then, while the call was on hold, they heard her talking with Terry in a normal voice, in which there was no trace of distress. At one point, she was heard asking her companion, "Where are those idiots? Are we still on hold?" When the sheriff's officer returned to the telephone, Carol once again began to sound like a normally worried wife.

Electing to testify, Carol put up a spirited fight in her own defense. She branded the babysitter an habitual liar, and firmly denied that she had ever offered Terry money to help kill her husband. She said she never planned or considered killing him. Instead, she portrayed herself as a loving wife and mother who was afraid of Terry, a much huskier and stronger woman. She said Terry had remarked that she "liked my body," and made repeated sexual advances toward her.

She claimed that Terry had carried out the murder on her own, had walked into the sleeping marine's bedroom and bludgeoned him, then threatened more violence if Carol tried to telephone for help.

She admitted helping Terry clean up the mess made by the bludgeoning and dress her husband, but insisted she acted under duress. She claimed the first time she knew anything about a murder was when Terry came out of the bedroom laughing.

"I saw her with the sash weight in hand. It was bloody," Carol testified.

She said Terry told her: "I just killed your husband, you bitch — for you."

Carol said she was then ordered to clean up the bedroom, while Terry sat down and drank a beer. She said she reached for the telephone to summon help, but "Terry waved that thing at me and told me I had kids in the other bedroom."

Asked by Deputy District Attorney Louis Boyle where in the bedroom she had seen blood, she sobbed and replied, "On the curtain, the ceiling, walls, floor, everywhere."

"Did you look at his head?" Boyle asked.

"Terry had made a remark not to look at him, it was a mess. His head was covered, thank God," she said.

Defense Attorney Donald Lewis argued that Terry had planned and committed the murder herself so that she and Carol would be free to carry on a lesbian love affair. He insisted that Terry controlled Carol's mind with fear, and described Terry as a heroin user, a confessed felon who wore a knife on her hip, and a braggart who boasted of shooting a policeman.

"This whole thing was conceived and carried out by Natha Mary DePew," he said.

The defense attorney told the jury that the young marine drill instructor was still alive, despite the beating, when he was taken from the house and Terry dumped him off the bridge.

During the state's summation Boyle drew the jury's attention to the tape recording, then called the defendant a liar and an accomplished actress.

"It is clear she is an actress, you heard it on the tape recording. Sobs, then a normal conversation, then sobs again," the assistant DA declared.

He said she had been caught in a number of lies, and then tried to explain her lies to the police by claiming that she had been threatened by her co-defendant. "But you heard the tape," he said. "There were no threats." Terry, he said, was "nothing but a tool used by Mrs. Hargis."

Boyle cautioned the jury not to permit defense arguments to cloud the case, and insisted that even if the victim was alive when he was driven away from the house, Carol was responsible for his death.

"She aided and abetted DePew," he declared, turning and glowering at the defendant. "The plan to kill him was premeditated and deliberate."

When the jury returned a verdict of guilty of first-degree murder, after only three hours' deliberation, Carol cried.

Approximately seven weeks later, she was sentenced by Judge Low to a life term in prison.

"This was a coldly planned-out killing, and she instigated it," the judge declared. "I tried to keep track during the trial of the numerous ways they discussed, and I lost track at ten or twelve.

"There were drugs in the beer, an electric cord in the shower, even one the co-defendant [Terry] remembered here on the stand — bullets in the carburetor. I never heard of that one before."

Both women were sent to the California Institution for Women in Frontera, California to serve their sentences.

CHAPTER EIGHT

THE SWINGING DENTIST

While many of the citizens of Greensboro, North Carolina were busy planning their Easter Sunday activities on a quiet early spring evening of 1986, one of their neighbors was guiding his car down the ramp into the police department's underground garage. His jumbled thoughts had nothing whatsoever to do with the rapidly approaching religious holiday.

As he spotted a policeman, he pulled to a stop and advised the startled officer: "I think I killed my wife and daughter."

The confrontation in the police garage marked the beginning of an investigation into one of the most grisly family murders in the often violent history of the North Carolina Piedmont.

Violence was not unknown in Greensboro. The bustling textile and insurance center had perhaps already seen far more than its fair share of senseless brutality: armed robberies, rapes, beatings and murders. And for two decades it was the scene of unusually ferocious racial and political conflicts.

The most savage of Greensboro's more than twenty years of stormy racial and political upheavals, exploded late in 1979 when five members and associates of the radical Communist Workers Party were shot to death in a one-sided gun battle and stick fight with a group of Ku Klux Klan, American Nazis and their supporters.

In recent years, hard work by determined community leaders and the dedicated efforts of a highly skilled and competent police department, had managed to prevent any serious new clashes on Greensboro's streets. But like police in every other city in the nation, they could only try their best to chip away at the more common forms of violence that afflicted their community, such as the explosive domestic battles that periodically flared between married — and unmarried — couples.

Even though domestic violence transcends all class distinctions, the man who confronted the policeman in the parking garage appeared to be about as untypical of Greensboro's more dangerous citizens as was possible.

Identifying himself as a local dentist, Jimmy Dale Hudson explained that he had been in a fight with his wife, Kay, and thought she was dead. He added that he was afraid their three-year-old daughter, Wilma Dale, might also be dead because she had "gotten in the way, somehow."

Hudson told police that his wife had flown into a rage, attacked him with a butcher knife, and slashed his neck, chest and hand before he was able to wrestle the weapon away from her. From that point onward, however, the dentist's memory either failed completely or, at best, became disturbingly spotty. He said he just couldn't remember everything that happened after he had won possession of the knife.

Despite his memory loss, Hudson seemed to be holding up well and to have himself under control. He scribbled on a piece of paper directions to the apartment his wife and daughter had moved to a few weeks earlier after they left him, and asked the officers to check on his family.

Police who rushed to the apartment a few blocks from the city's Ben L. Smith High School found that it had been turned into a slaughterhouse.

In the foyer, just inside the front door, investigators found the body of the little girl sprawled in a messy pool of blood and excrement. The child was wearing a pink nightgown, with a brown coat thrown over it as if she had been hurriedly dressed to leave the apartment. Valentine cards and a toy car were stuffed into the coat's pockets. So much blood covered the nightgown that only small bits of the garment's original pink coloring could be discerned.

The blood came from an ugly gaping wound that had almost completely severed Wilma Dale's neck. An autopsy conducted later by the Guilford County Coroner in nearby Chapel Hill disclosed that her neck had been cut with two deep slashes that sliced all the way to her spine, almost decapitating her.

Inside the living room, an Easter Egg dyeing kit was scattered on the floor, and a few feet away, the body of Kay Hudson was sprawled face up between a recliner and an antique bar. The blue-jean-clad woman's legs were splayed, and like her daughter, her head had been nearly sliced from her body. A bloody handkerchief was stuffed into the wound that almost completely girdled her neck laying the flesh open all the way to her spine.

Strangely, for an area where such violence had so recently occurred, the neatly kept apartment appeared barely disturbed. The television was on, and in the kitchen, a pan of muffins was still cooling on the counter.

In the kitchen, officers found a blood-covered butcher knife lying on the floor, and a blood-stained rolling pin and spatula were found inside a closed kitchen drawer. Laboratory tests later revealed that the stains on the knife matched Mrs. Hudson's blood type. The stains on the other implements matched her husband's blood type.

A .38-caliber pistol was also found in the apartment, and police confiscated another loaded and bloodstained .38 from Hudson's car.

After the police photographed the positions of the bodies in the apartment and completed other phases of the on-scene investigation, the remains of the mother and daughter were removed and scheduled for autopsies.

Hudson was taken to the Wesley Long Community Hospital, where he was treated for minor lacerations, then locked in the Guilford County Jail. It was March 24 — six days before Easter, but police and prosecutors involved in the investigation had little time for thoughts of the religious holiday. Instead, they began looking into the backgrounds of the suspected killer and his victims, seeking clues to explain the behavior and events, that led to the tragic destruction of a family.

They learned that Jimmy Dale Hudson and Kathryn (Kay) Everett were college sweethearts who met at the University of North Carolina in Chapel Hill. Jimmy earned undergraduate and dental degrees there — he was a Phi Beta Kappa honors graduate. Kay graduated in 1971 with a degree in dental hygiene.

The daughter of a Baptist minister, Kay was born in Yazoo City, Mississippi. Like Kay, Jimmy wasn't a native Tarheel. He was born in Georgia, but he and his parents moved to Greensboro before he was old enough for high school. His father went to work in the local textile mills and Jimmy began proving his mettle as a scholar, graduating as an honor student at Page High School, before moving on to the university — and meeting Kay.

Kay was pretty and bright, and soon after

she and Jimmy met they were attending Sunday services together at the First Baptist Church in Greensboro, where they were later married.

After graduation from college, the young couple moved to Robbinsville, a quiet mountain community in the western part of the state near the Tennessee border, where Jimmy set up his first practice as a dentist, with Kay working as dental hygienist. The young dentist quickly developed a reputation for good work, and he and Kay would later be remembered there as having worked well together.

Four years after settling in Robbinsville, the Hudsons moved to Greensboro and Jimmy joined two other dentists in a shared practice. Kay became involved as a partner in a local consulting firm and began taking courses in business administration at the Greensboro campus of the University of North Carolina. When she was needed, however, Kay continued to fill in as a hygienist for her husband.

The young dentist was generally regarded by those who knew him as an amiable, even-tempered, hard-working professional man who depended heavily on his wife. In fact, there were indications that he, perhaps, depended on her too much. It was Kay who had encouraged him to become a dentist, and it was she who kept the books when he established his dental practice. She also designed their first home in Robbinsville. Despite his intelligence, scholarship and industry, Hudson had grown up as a spoiled mama's boy. He was an only child, born late in the lives of his parents, and both father and mother doted on him. He was so close to his mother, that he slept in the same bed with her until he was fifteen years old, while his hard-drinking father slept on a roll-away bed. In marriage, Hudson transferred his dependence and need for almost constant attention to his wife. Kay was devoted to him and put up with his demands, as well as his refusal to help with even the simplest household chores. And as he spent more and more time with private activities she busied herself with her studies.

Hudson had a penchant for guns and trains, and liked to involve himself in the activities at the University of North Carolina. He became a member of the Rams Club, which was composed of well-to-do donors to the University's athletic program. He fixed the players' teeth and often visited them in the locker rooms. He also began taking long railroad trips across the country, a few times with Kay, but more often without her. And he had collected from fifteen to twenty guns which he kept in the house.

Strains on the marriage intensified when Hudson started pursuing other women, and made sexual advances toward a close relative of his wife. In 1983, Greensboro police had investigated death threats against him for sleeping with another man's girlfriend. Much later it was reported by a psychiatrist in court testimony that Hudson wanted sex ten times a week.

In April 1983, after thirteen years of a childless marriage because Kay was unable to conceive, the Hudsons adopted Wilma Dale from the North Carolina Children's Home Society. Respected in the community, well-educated and financially well-off, they seemed to be perfectly qualified to become adoptive parents. A friend who worked for the Guilford (County) Department of Social Services had coached the couple on questions they would likely be asked to determine their suitability as parents.

Kay was thrilled with her daughter. Jimmy Dale was jealous! The little girl had respiratory problems, earaches, sore throats, and the usual childhood ailments. As the time Kay spent caring for her daughter increased, time her husband felt deprived him of her attention, he realized he didn't like sharing his wife.

"How can you have a marriage and a child?" he reportedly once groused to a relative.

As children do, when Wilma Dale was sick, or wanted attention, she sometimes cried, and as she reached the toddler stage, she began getting into things. Hudson's irritation with the child mounted, displayed by his refusal to call her by name. Instead, he referred to her as "the child."

Meanwhile the swinging dentist's trips and womanizing had caused his work to suffer. He began taking too many days off from the dental office, and even when he did show up, his work was no longer up to its previous quality. Upset and concerned, his colleagues finally severed their relationship with him and Jimmy

Dale suddenly found himself without a dental practice.

Just as she had been determined to be a good wife, Kay was determined to be a good mother, but her husband's jealousy of Wilma Dale sparked repeated disputes, and his sexual behavior became more and more outrageous. His business troubles magnified his childlike dependence on her and she began to realize that the marriage could not be saved. She knew he was having affairs because she had found in his briefcase copies of love letters he had written to women. When he asked her to join him at a nudist camp, she refused, and there were other escapades she didn't even want to discuss.

Finally, early in March, 1986, her patience snapped. Her husband was away on a Caribbean vacation without his wife and daughter. Sometime before leaving he had pleaded: "Kay, you have to find a way to get rid of [Wilma] Dale."

"I did," she confided to a close friend. "The only thing is, I went with her."

When Jimmy Dale returned from his sun-and-fun vacation, he walked into an empty house. Kay had left a letter: "Always know that I care very much about you, and that is why I am not here. The pain you were in last Sunday seemed like gangrene caused by our relationship and amputation is the only healing process available..." she wrote.

"I have tried to work, provide a home, a

child, support, and sex, but something that I do just seems to create a very unhappy dependent response in you. I have tried to be tolerant of your girlfriends...I have loved you for seventeen years, but I cannot continue to watch you in pain."

She said that now that he was free of his dental practice, she felt he should be free of her and Wilma Dale, as well. "I want you to be happy. It is all I have ever wanted," she wrote. Finally, showing her concern — and uneasy forebodings of danger — she cautioned, "If you think of being violent to yourself or to others, remember that life is a precious gift and not yours to take away."

The mother and daughter moved to a small two-story apartment, and Kay began the job of rebuilding their lives. She had recently completed her master's degree in business administration, and after teaching college part time, had just accepted a new job at the Moses Cone Memorial Hospital. She told Greensboro psychologist Dr. John Edwards, who counselled the couple while their marriage was crumbling around them, that she planned to begin dating other men. "I have no intention of moving back," she declared.

Jimmy panicked. Throughout their marriage, he had depended on the super-efficient Kay to make almost all of his family and business decisions. No matter what the nature of his troubles, or how outrageous his behavior, Kay had always been there to lean on. She had even made the funeral and burial arrangements when his father and mother died, because he was too grief-stricken to deal with the details himself.

Jimmy Dale began calling on members of Kay's family, pleading for their help in bringing about a reconciliation. He repeatedly telephoned Kay's aunt in California, to whom he admitted his romantic escapades, and also confessed that he knew he had not behaved properly toward Wilma Dale. He promised to change.

He also bitterly complained, however, that Kay had gotten an education, a car and a new job, then deserted him. "I used to think Kay was a warm, loving person. And now I see that she's a cold, calculating woman," the aunt later recalled him saying.

During a meeting with Dr. Edwards, about two weeks before the slayings, Kay asked him to counsel her husband and warned that Jimmy Dale might become violent. "If he kills himself, he won't go alone," she said. She added that she was fearful for her husband's safety, and for the safety of her parents. She also talked about his need for love affairs to gratify his ego, and of his jealousy of her job and of Wilma Dale, which he considered rivals for her time and affection.

In a brief period of about a month, the thirty-eight-year-old Jimmy Dale Hudson, who had always seemed to be a winner, had lost his business and was in the process of losing his wife. Kay told Dr. Edwards that her husband had begun talking about mass murder. And only three weeks after Kay fled with Wilma Dale from their comfortable Oak Ridge home to sanctuary in the little rental apartment, the mother and daughter were dead.

In a statement to police, Jimmy Dale said that he and his wife had enjoyed a normal marriage with "a few rough spots." He conceded that he had engaged in several affairs with other women, although never with anyone in Greensboro because he was concerned about his reputation in the community. And he told of once asking Kay to visit a nudist colony with him. She refused the nudist colony proposal, he stated. "She finally just told me to do my thing, but don't bring home any pregnant women or diseases. As far as I am aware, Kay never had any affairs with anyone."

He said that on the day of the slayings, he visited with Wilma Dale for several hours, then dropped her off at Kay's apartment about 6 P.M. When Kay asked him to leave, however, he objected and asked to kiss Wilma Dale goodbye because he did not know how long it would be before he would see her again. Jimmy Dale related that the little girl had come downstairs in her nightgown, put her winter coat on because she was cold, and he had held her in his arms.

He said Kay was afraid he was trying to take the child out of the house and they began quarreling, which upset Wilma Dale who began to cry.

"I sat down on the floor at the foot of the stairs and was holding Dale. Then all of a sudden, Kay slapped me two or three times," he claimed. "Then she hit me with something and the next thing I knew, Kay had a butcher knife. Kay aimed at me with the knife. That's when I got cut on the hand. That's when, I guess, two people got crazy and violent at the same time."

Hudson said, the next thing he remembered was being in the kitchen washing blood from his hands. He said he remembered seeing the bodies of his wife and daughter — one in the living room and the other in the foyer. After taking his shirt off and dropping it on the kitchen floor (investigators found it in the foyer), he drove to the police department, he said. Authorities later determined that approximately two hours had expired between the time of the murders and his appearance in the police parking garage.

Coupled with his complaints of partial memory loss about important details of the slayings, were later claims he made of hearing strange disembodied voices, and remarks supposedly addressed to him from God.

Hudson was indicted on two counts of first-degree murder. Assistant District Attorney Gary Goodman, who was assigned the case along with Assistant District Attorney Rick Greeson announced that he was prepared to seek the death penalty. According to North Carolina law, when deliberating between life in prison or the death penalty, the jury would be permitted to consider the cruelty of the attack and the fact that there were two victims.

Goodman was quoted in the *Greensboro News & Record* as predicting that states' evidence might show that the mother and daughter had suffered slow deaths and that one might have witnessed the other's murder.

As Hudson remained in custody, first in the Guilford County Jail in Greensboro, then across the state in the Eastern Correctional Center at Maury, where he was undergoing psychiatric testing and waiting for trial, he announced that he hoped to receive the death sentence. But his lawyer, Greensboro attorney Michael Schlosser, revealed that he was considering the use of an insanity defense, and pointed to Hudson's pleas for the death penalty as evidence of mental imbalance.

Then early in 1987, less than two weeks before the case was scheduled to go to trial, a new attorney for Hudson filed legal motions in Guilford Superior Court claiming that Assistant DA Goodman had improperly linked criminal plea negotiations to a civil lawsuit by refusing to honor a plea bargain agreement.

Raleigh attorney Thomas C. Manning, who was more experienced in insanity defenses and death penalty cases than was his predecessor, charged that Goodman, the prosecutor, had agreed to permit Hudson to plead guilty to two counts of second-degree murder in exchange for a prison sentence of one hundred years. However, Manning said Goodman withdrew his agreement after civil attorneys handling the $2.2 million wrongful death lawsuit filed by Kay's father against Hudson's estate were unable to get together on a settlement.

The prosecutor had improperly involved himself in a civil matter and used criminal plea negotiations as a bargaining tool to speed up a settlement in the civil suit, the Raleigh attorney claimed. And he asked that the prosecution be required to honor the plea-bargain agreement.

In another legal move, Manning also charged that the prosecutor's statements to the media had damaged his client's rights to a fair trial. And he asked the court to dismiss the murder indictments against Hudson because of what he said was "prosecutorial misconduct."

Goodman countered that his statements quoted in the news article reiterated information that had already been made public at a bond hearing. And in regard to the plea-bargain flap, he said he had not accepted the offer discussed with attorney Schlosser because the agreement was not in writing. He conceded that he didn't tell Schlosser he was rejecting the proposal. "I didn't think I had to," he said.

Superior Court Judge Tom Ross denied the move for dismissal of the indictments, ruling that Goodman's statements to the press had not endangered Hudson's right to a fair trial.

Judge Ross also rejected the defense lawyer's effort to make the prosecution honor the proposed plea bargain arrangement. He ruled that "there was not a meeting of the minds," between Goodman and Schlosser, and consequently no agreement had been reached.

A few weeks later, a settlement was reached in the wrongful death lawsuit filed by Kay's father. The terms were sealed by court order, but a judge later permitted disclosure. In the settlement, Jimmy Dale agreed to relinquish ownership of homes in Oak Ridge and Robbinsville, as well as property in Ocean Isle Beach, $23,500 in bank accounts, and an undisclosed amount of stocks and bonds, life insurance policies and trust accounts. He was permitted to retain slightly more than $100,000 from a federal retirement program and his dental pension plan to pay for his defense in the civil and criminal cases.

In a much more generous agreement reached between the husband and wife nine days after their separation and only ten days before the slayings, the dentist would have retained the home in Oak Ridge, vehicles, corporate stock and his valuable model railroad collection.

By the time the settlement in the civil lawsuit was reached, selection of a jury for Hudson's criminal trial had already begun. Almost a year earlier, after psychiatric evaluation, Hudson had been declared fit to stand trial.

As the trial opened, Manning wasted no time outlining the game plan, asserting that his client was insane when the twin slayings occurred, and, therefore, not criminally responsible. In opening statements, he told the jury that a mental ailment had filled Jimmy Dale's mind with "the seeds of something that could cause an incident like this to happen and which did happen."

Only three hours before Hudson slashed his wife and child to death, he was in the office of Dr. Edwards taking tests that revealed a personality disorder serious enough to cause psychotic behavior, Manning revealed.

In the prosecution's opening statement, Assistant DA Goodman told the jury about Hudson's appearance at the police department, and of the account the dentist provided of his fears he had killed Kay and the child during a quarrel. Hudson claimed Kay attacked him with a butcher knife and cut him on the neck, chest and hand before he could disarm her, the assistant DA said. And he advised the jury of Hudson's claims that he couldn't remember what had happened after he won control of the weapon.

Goodman also informed the jury of seven women and five men that they would be asked to look at gruesome photographs of the murder victims. Manning had pleaded with the judge to severely limit the number of photographs admitted as evidence, arguing that they were repetitive and could inflame the jury against the defendant. Goodman claimed, however, that introduction of each of the photographs, which showed the victims both at the scene of the twin slaying and during the autopsies, was necessary to support the testimony of pathologists, who would be describing the wounds, their placement on the bodies and their effect. He pointed out that the photographs would clearly show facial bruising, thereby revealing publicly for the first time that both Kay and

Wilma Dale had apparently been beaten before they were slashed to death. The prosecutor contended that the pictures should not be excluded from evidence merely because they were horrifying and revolting.

Judge Rose ruled that the photographs could be admitted, marking up what experienced courtroom observers considered to be an important early triumph for the prosecution in its effort to win not only a conviction, but the death penalty.

The jury was also permitted to view a gory police department videotape of the death scene, showing the bloody bodies, their grotesque wounds, the bloodstains and scuff marks inside the apartment. The relatively undisturbed condition of furniture and other items in the apartment, as shown in the tapes, was important to the prosecution's efforts to uncover holes in Hudson's claim of a violent struggle with his wife over the butcher knife.

Color photos were used as well to illustrate the shallow wounds and scratches Hudson claimed were injuries he suffered as the result of the knife attack by his infuriated wife. A hospital emergency room physician who treated Hudson testified that the neck injuries were probably caused by fingernails and not by a knife, and that the hand and chest lacerations were the result of slashing motions rather than stabbing movements. The doctor said Hudson was calm during his treatment and examination, and did not mention his wife or child.

Evidence was later admitted showing there were no holes made by cutting or stabbing in the T-shirt Hudson was wearing when he surrendered to police, or in a blue shirt investigators believed he had on when the slayings occurred. The shirt, smeared with Kay's blood, but not with her husband's, was found in the entrance way near the stairwell to the second-floor bedrooms.

Pathologists provided some of the most grisly testimony of the trial, and Dr. James M. Sullivan told the jury that Hudson's wife was beaten so brutally that she may have already been unconscious when her throat was slashed. The neck wound was inflicted with such force that her major arteries and windpipe were severed, and the blade of the weapon sliced into her neck bone.

Wilma Dale may have been conscious when her neck was slashed so severely that the wound opened her flesh halfway to her backbone, Dr. Robert L. Thompson, another pathologist, testified. And there were indications that the mortally wounded child may even have taken a few steps after the dreadful attack. Under questioning by Manning, Thompson did concede that it was conceivable that Wilma Kay could have been struck by accident.

Assistant DA Goodman, however, made the point that the doctor's testimony did not indicate an accidental stabbing. And the prosecutor noted that Wilma Kay was not stabbed, but instead was slashed with what the lacerations to her spine indicated were at least two cutting or slashing motions.

The photographs also showed that the bodies were in different rooms, about 30 feet apart. Bits of Jimmy Dale's hair were found on Wilma Dale's clothing and body, and an FBI expert testified that one of the hairs had been forcibly pulled from his head.

FBI analysis of bloodstain patterns at the crime scene were also stressed by the prosecution in efforts to defuse Jimmy Dale's contention that the child could have been killed accidentally when she got in the way of her struggling parents. Samples definitely matching Wilma Dale's blood type were found only in the pool of blood on and surrounding her body in the entrance way to the apartment, and on and around the butcher knife police found on the kitchen floor. Other stains in the entrance way, kitchen, bathroom and living room either matched samples of Jimmy Dale's, Kay's blood type or were of undetermined origin.

The trial had been underway several days when the prosecution dropped twin bombshells. Greeson disclosed that library records from the Central Prison showed that the former college honors student had spent much of his time in custody studying everything he could learn about an insanity defense. Introduced by Greeson immediately after Jimmy Dale had testified he knew little about an insanity defense, other than what he had learned from his attorneys, the revelation made a startling impact.

On the stand the defendant lamely responded to the disclosure of his research activities by declaring: "It has in no way influenced me in telling the truth as I remember it. It was part of my self-psychotherapy."

Possibly even more damaging to his efforts to avoid the death penalty, if convicted, was testimony from another inmate at the Eastern Correctional Center, a prison law librarian, who told the jury that the defendant had admitted slaying his wife — then took twenty minutes to think it over before slashing Wilma Dale's throat.

Roger McQueen, serving life for the execution-style slaying of two prostitutes, said it was disgust at Hudson's disclosure of the ruthless slaying of the little girl that prompted him to risk harm from other inmates by cooperating with authorities.

McQueen, who had built a reputation at the prison in Maury as a savvy self-taught jailhouse lawyer after spending more than 23 of his 48 years behind bars, said Jimmy Dale admitted that Wilma Dale witnessed Kay's murder, and that he sent her from the room. McQueen quoted him as saying that he later held the sobbing child in his arms and comforted her, before nearly decapitating her with the knife.

"He said the kid was not his and he had to kill the baby to make it fit," McQueen declared.

The prosecutors also disclosed that not only

had Jimmy Dale been a frequenter of nudist camps and an unfaithful husband but that he had traveled hundreds of miles to participate in group sex and had also made homosexual overtures to other men. The prosecutors produced boxes of sexually explicit photographs and love letters, much of it found under his bed by police, as evidence of his behavior.

Jimmy Dale reluctantly admitted that he had advertised in swinger or wife-swapping magazines. But when he testified that Kay had also participated in the activities, he was confronted with letters and previous statements in which he said he did not believe his wife was unfaithful and complained about her refusal to join him as a swinger.

The defendant, who had sat at the defense table with his head bowed toward an open Bible, showed his discomfort during the questioning and claimed that his sexual peccadillos were not a large part of his life and had nothing to do with the murders.

"It's just sad that all this material has to be discussed," he said.

Nevertheless, during a grueling three days of testimony, he was repeatedly caught in lies, and forced to admit to his busy sex life and spirited correspondence with single women and couples across the country.

Greeson also hit hard at the bizarre supernatural experiences Jimmy Dale claimed he had undergone, which included hallucinations and the contemplation of suicide.

Jimmy Dale told the jury that shortly after

his wife left him, he visited the cemetery where his parents were buried and his father spoke to him from the grave. "Pardner, you've made mistakes. Go tell her you love her," the spectral voice reputedly advised him. Jimmy Dale also said that God had appeared to him as a "warm glowing presence" and offered similar advice.

Although the troubled dentist insisted that shortly after the slayings he had tried to kill himself in his car by firing a bullet into his head, Greeson pointed out he had somehow failed in the point-blank suicide attempt. Nor could investigators find any bullet holes in the vehicle. Jimmy Dale said that at another time he considered getting a friend to smuggle cyanide to him in the jail, but did not carry through with the plan.

Early in the proceedings a defense psychiatrist, Dr. Selwyn Rose, of nearby Winston-Salem, had testified that he believed the defendant was insane when the murders occurred and was suffering a "psychotic episode." "You paint him as a cold-blooded killer," the expert witness declared. "In fact, he's a wimp."

Rose, who is also a lawyer and has testified in hundreds of trials, was one of four psychiatrists and a psychologist who took the stand to say that Jimmy Dale was insane when the mother and daughter were slain.

Only one psychiatrist, Dr. Bob Rollings of the Dorothy Dix Psychiatric Hospital in Raleigh, N.C., testified that he believed Jimmy Dale was sane when his wife and child were killed. Dr. Rollins, who had examined Hudson at the hospital shortly after the slayings, told the jury that after the dentist's wife — on whom he had been extremely dependent — left him, he had flown into a violent rage.

Five weeks after the trial began, testimony was concluded.

Defense attorneys claimed in closing arguments that the very savagery of the assault on the mother and child was proof of their client's insanity. "You can take the ferocity of the wounds with what the doctors say, then I think there is a compelling inference that can be made that he was out of control," Manning insisted to the jury.

Calling on the jury to return with verdicts of first-degree murder, Greeson said of Wilma Dale: "He executed that young lady, just like he did his wife. It's as much as a signature."

The jury deliberated thirteen hours before returning verdicts of first-degree murder in Wilma Dale's slaying, and second-degree murder in Kay's death. Jimmy Dale listened stonefaced as the verdicts were read.

Four days later, after a hard-fought sentencing hearing in the first-degree murder of Wilma Dale, the same jury decided against the death penalty and recommended that he be sentenced to life in prison.

Judge Ross ordered a life term for Wilma Dale's slaying, and another fifty-year-term for Kay's killing. Defense attorneys argued that their client should be given no more than fifteen years for the murder of his wife. But the judge ruled that the defendant had perjured himself, in particular when he claimed that his knowledge of the insanity defense was solely based on talks with his lawyers, and cited that as an aggravating factor justifying the stiffer sentence.

Jimmy Dale is expected to be eligible for parole in about forty years.

CHAPTER NINE

PRISONERS OF LOVE

When Constable Cletus A'Hearne of the Royal Canadian Mounted Police was summoned at 1:15 A.M. to a middle-class neighborhood in Winnipeg, Manitoba, it seemed to be a routine call.

Even after A'Hearne was shown the dead body of a nude young man sprawled face down across the sidewalk, and had taken a statement from the victim's widow, there didn't appear to be much evidence that this particular tragedy was any different than many others the RCMP was called in to investigate.

The dead man, his body partially covered by a coat someone had thoughtfully draped over him, was John Bruce Down, a twenty-five-year-old electrician with the Royal Canadian

Air Force. A veteran of the Korean conflict, Down was married to a nurse at the Deer Lodge Hospital and they were the parents of two little girls.

As A'Hearne and other officers worked in the Spring darkness to piece together the elements of the tragedy, it appeared that a terrible accident had occurred. A second-story window to Down's bedroom directly overlooked the stretch of sidewalk and flower patch where the body lay, and the victim's widow Katie, pointed out to investigators that her husband had been a frequent sleepwalker.

It seemed conceivable that Down had been walking in his sleep, and tumbled out the window to his death.

Although Katie wasn't crying, A'Hearne found her to be emotionally upset, as would be expected of any woman whose husband had just been killed. But, as the constable later noted in a written report, she gave him "the impression she more or less expected this."

However, if the investigators had known more about the recent history of the Down's three-year-old marriage, they might have been more curious about the widow's apparent expectation of tragedy.

Gerald Ford, a childhood friend who grew up with John Down in Newfoundland, and his wife, Tina, had visited with the couple for several hours the evening before the young airman's death. Down had been in a good mood and talked animatedly about buying a station wagon and loading up his family for a drive to Newfoundland later in the summer.

As the talk progressed, however, someone had asked Katie if she planned to have additional children. "Not by that man," she had snapped, turning to look at her husband. Down had passed the remark off as a joke, and had remained in a pleasant mood until the guests had left.

It's doubtful, however, that Down could have maintained his lighthearted attitude had he known how troubled his marriage really was: Katie had been carrying on a torrid affair for six months with a hard-drinking womanizer who was an orderly at the hospital where she worked, and their romantic trysts had been carried on in the hospital's laundry room.

Fourteen years older than the twenty-four-year-old nurse, Alexander George "Sandy" Harper was not only a demanding lover, but could also be violent, especially when he had been drinking.

John Down had barely been lowered into his grave before Sandy moved firmly into the lives of the widow and her daughters. A neighbor, who was also an employee at the Deer Lodge Hospital, saw him at the Down house a few days after the airman's death. She had never forgotten how puzzled she was by Katie's composure when she called to offer condolences to the new widow.

Even before John Down's death, another neighbor had seen Sandy at the house when the young husband had been hospitalized for minor surgery on his nose. While eating breakfast and idly looking through her kitchen window, the neighbor had seen a shirtless man walk downstairs in the Down house. Later Katie had introduced the same man to her as Sandy Harper.

John Down's siblings were also surprised at the new widow's composure after they met her for the first time in Newfoundland where she travelled for his funeral.

They later remembered that she offered sleeping pills to family members during the distressing period of the wake and funeral. While reminiscing in the kitchen about John, one of the brothers became very distressed and Katie had suggested that he be given a sleeping capsule with holes punched into the casing to make the medication work faster. When he refused, Down's sister, Sylvia, later declared under oath, that Katie finally emptied a capsule into his coffee while he wasn't looking.

A forensic pathologist at the Winnipeg General Hospital conducted the autopsy on the body a few hours after Down's death. A report of the autopsy, along with samples of major organs, were submitted to the RCMP. A'Hearne asked for tests at the RCMP laboratory in Regina for barbiturates, alcohol, heavy metals or poisons, and samples of the organs were subsequently forwarded to the laboratory.

On the day of the inquest, the pathologist received a report based on the laboratory studies in Regina indicating there were two levels of sodium amytal in blood from the liver. Sodium amytal is a barbiturate that is easily detectable by its bitter taste. In view of the report, which contradicted the pathologist's initial tests, the death was officially attributed to a combination of the barbiturate and to concussion from the fall. Down had dropped backward from the window, and blood from abrasions on his back indicated he had still been alive when he fell, the pathologist determined. Suicide, or a sleepwalking accident, was cited as the immediate cause.

Less than fifteen months after John Down died, his widow and Sandy Harper were married. It would become a marriage made in Hell — a marriage later described as a life of mutual blackmail.

Katie gave birth to another daughter after she and Sandy were married about a year, and his son and daughter by a previous marriage visited often. The son, Norman Alexander Harper, moved in with them for a while when he was sixteen.

But the presence of a houseful of children offered no guarantee of happiness. Sandy continued his heavy boozing and he and Katie quarrelled constantly. The girls grew used to awakening at night to the sounds of screams and violence. Katie's daughters quickly learned to run to their mother for shelter when Sandy was drinking, and avoided their stepfather whenever possible. Norman, who was older than the girls, would later describe his father as "slap happy" when he was drinking.

At various times Katie's oldest daughter, Patricia Kathleen, asked her mother why she didn't leave Sandy. Katie always replied with the same answer or a close variation: "I can't leave right now. My life depends on it. I'll tell you later."

By 1976 the stormy relationship between the two onetime lovers had reached its breaking point. They split up and Sandy moved out of the house. As they were no longer employed at the hospital, they seldom saw one another. Sandy had found a job as a janitor, and Katie had spent most of the last ten years working as an embalmer at a local funeral home.

Shortly after the split, his face a mass of bruises, Sandy showed up at the home of his daughter, Denise. He claimed that one of his stepdaughter's boyfriends had beaten him up in order to force him to give his half of the house to Katie.

Sandy was unaware that the boyfriend had been talking to the RCMP about stories he had heard from Katie. Most of the details of the boyfriend's conversation with the officers were never disclosed in court, but he revealed enough to rekindle RCMP interest in the curious death of John Down. The Mounties reopened the case and asked Katie to come into their headquarters for a talk and a session with the lie detector.

Finally Katie had had enough of her life with Sandy. Once she started talking, her version of the events that had occurred during the night of her husband's death 17 long years ago, tumbled out of her in a torrent.

She admitted doctoring John's coffee with three sleeping pills, so that he fell asleep soon after their friends left and before Sandy arrived at the house. She said Sandy wanted sex, and when she protested that it was too dangerous because her husband was upstairs asleep, her lover told her: "I'll fix that."

According to her account, she followed as Sandy climbed the stairs to her husband's bedroom, and watched as he smothered the sleeping man with a pillow. Then she and Sandy returned downstairs and made love. After the lovemaking session, they went upstairs again and she helped Sandy push her husband's nude body out the window.

"I'll never forget the thud as long as I live," Katie told her interrogators. She said she had lived in fear of Sandy ever since her first husband was killed.

Ironically, police couldn't use Katie's damning confession against Sandy because the couple were still husband and wife. But they could use it against her, and in October 1977, eighteen years after her first husband died, Katie was charged with his murder. With the filing of the charges, legal precedent was set in Canada because of the lengthy time lapse since John Down's death. A Crown spokesman was quoted in the press as saying the only comparable case he could locate occurred in seventeenth-century England.

It was eleven months later, and Katie was forty-four before she was finally brought to trial in Winnipeg's austere law courts building. The terrible secret she had lived with for nearly half her life would at last be publicly revealed.

A'Hearne, now retired from the RCMP, was one of the witnesses, and he testified that he had been suspicious of John Down's death since the first few minutes he spent at the scene. "I wasn't satisfied...that this man had jumped and died," he said.

Other testimony indicated that a high level of sodium amytal had been found in the body, and the Crown pointed out that Katie had been a nurse at Deer Lodge where she had easy access to the powerful sleeping potion. Her former neighbor also testified to seeing Sandy, stripped to the waist, at the Down home while the airman was still alive but hospitalized.

During the gruelling seven-day trial Katie watched and listened impassively as the testimony and evidence mounted against her. Her defense attorney Lawrence Greenberg attempted to show that it was her fear of Sandy after his brutal murder of her husband and his threats to her that had kept her silent all those years. But she did not take the stand. The Crown called 26 witnesses. Greenberg declined to call any defense witnesses whatsoever.

During his summation Greenberg conceded that although his client had proven "beyond doubt that she's a liar and an adulterer," that did not mean she was a murderer. "Sandy

Harper was the perpetrator of this heinous crime," Greenberg declared.

Crown counsel George Dangerfield contended that in 1976 Katie had decided it was time to get rid of Sandy Harper by accusing him of a terrible murder, just as in 1959, she had decided to get rid of John Down, because she was involved in "a triangle, a disappointing marriage, a husband she no longer loved — a perfect mixture for murder."

The eight-man, four-woman jury deliberated nine hours, and then returned a verdict of guilty of capital murder. Katie was sentenced to the mandatory term of life in prison. In actual practice, the sentence meant she would not be eligible for parole until the year 2003 when she was sixty-nine. She was sent to the prison for women in Kingston, Ontario.

But the bizarre saga of Katie and Sandy Harper and the curious murder of John Down hadn't yet played its course.

After losing a petition to the Manitoba Court of Appeal for a new trial, Katie took her case to the Supreme Court of Canada. In December 1980 the justices ruled unanimously to grant her a new trial. The court ruled that the trial judge had erred in not determining the voluntariness of the statement she gave to police, before admitting it as evidence. Katie was released on bail a few days before Christmas and spent the holiday with her family. She had served a little more than two years behind bars.

A few weeks later in January 1981, she and Sandy were named in a new joint indictment preferred by the attorney general of Manitoba, which accused them of the murder of John Down twenty-two years earlier. It was the first time Sandy had been charged in the homicide, although he had been named as a possible accessory in the original indictment prepared against Katie in October 1977. He was quietly taken into custody at his home in Winnipeg.

More than a year elapsed between preparation of the indictment and the trial. The delay was partly caused by the type of legal maneuvering that is part of any important criminal or civil case. One of the knottiest points of contention was the Crown's insistence on a joint murder trial, a proposal opposed by attorneys for both the defendants. Some of the delay, however, was due to health problems Katie had developed. Some news reports erroneously indicated that she was expected to undergo surgery for lung cancer, but it was later learned that the surgery was tied to tuberculosis which she had developed during her stay in prison.

At last, in February 1982, Katie appeared again for the new trial ordered by the Supreme Court. She was now forty-eight, and a grandmother of five. Her heavily lined face and skinny form clearly showed the effects of the surgery she had so recently undergone, and of the past years' ordeal. This time, Sandy, a rumpled and wrinkled sixty-two, was her co-defendant, and as they sat quietly, side-by-side in the prisoner's dock, the estranged husband and wife never spoke or even looked at one another. Each of them had provided police statements blaming the other for the slaying.

In his opening statement, Crown Attorney Dangerfield promised a jury of seven men and five women that he would show that the defendants killed Katie's first husband because he was an obstacle to their continuing love affair.

"I intend to prove that the plan executed was the cold-blooded and deliberate murder of John Down," he declared. Dangerfield said witnesses would prove that Down was drugged by Katie, smothered by Sandy, then pushed from his bedroom window by the pair to make it appear he had tumbled outside while sleep-walking or while under the influence of barbiturates.

Dr. George Mulligan, an expert in the study of injuries, testified that cyanosis, a bluish coloring in the victim's upper body, led him to conclude that Down was probably strangled or smothered before plunging through the window.

The traumatologist and head of Manitoba's accident and research center conceded, however, that except for the presence of the cyanosis there was also a possibility that Down could have been killed in the fall by a brain stem concussion that stopped his breathing.

Dr. Mulligan said his investigation indicated Down went out of the window backwards, fell to the pitch part of the roof, slid on his back to the eave, then dropped to the sidewalk. The doctor discounted the possibility of sleepwalking as a factor in the death.

Testifying once again, A'Hearne said the initial autopsy report he received three days after the victim's death showed no traces of barbiturates in the body. But a corrected report received several weeks later from the RCMP laboratory in Regina disclosed low levels of barbiturates, and A'Hearne revealed that Down's stomach had somehow been lost during the autopsy. The pathologist testified that although he couldn't recall that the stomach had been lost, it was possible because after so many years it was difficult to remember the details of the case.

The pathologist also testified that on the day of the inquest he received a report contradicting his initial tests and indicating low levels of sodium amytal in blood from the victim's liver. "...I concluded that in view of the uncertainty of barbiturate levels, I was forced to attribute death to a combination of the barbiturate and the concussion of the fall," he said of the inquest.

William Radych, senior chemist in charge of toxicology at the RCMP crime detection laboratory in 1959, provided startling testimony by disclosing that he had made a mistake twenty-two years earlier when he determined that Down had died with a near fatal amount of drugs in his system.

Radych said he had recalculated his results — and only four days before being called to testify, discovered that the level of drugs in Down's body may have been within the therapeutic limit.

"In checking results this week I found I had made a mathematical error. I realized I had used two different solution standards in comparing the blood and urine samples," the chemist reported. His surprise testimony appeared to damage the Crown's case against Katie.

Once again, the Fords testified about their visit with the Downs the night their friend died, and about Katie's remark that she didn't plan to have any more children with John. However, under cross examination by her attorney, Gerald Ford conceded that she could have been joking when she made the remark.

Some of the trial's most dramatic testimony came from members of the defendants' families who, sometimes tearfully, related stories of the emotional, physical and sexual abuse they had suffered in the couple's household.

One of the witnesses told the jury that Sandy had confessed to helping push Down's body out the window, but had placed most of the blame for the incident on Katie. Sandy claimed that Katie had telephoned him early on June 1, 1959 and asked him to come to her apartment. According to his story, when he got there, Down had been drugged, although Sandy didn't know what kind of medication had been used. Sandy admitted that he then placed a pillow over the unconscious man's face, the witness continued, but claimed he couldn't go through with the murder and returned downstairs.

So Katie climbed the stairs, "and did, whatever," Sandy was quoted as saying. He then went back up and helped put the body out the window, the witness testified.

Sandy's son, Norman Alexander Harper, told the court that he was fifteen when he was awakened by the sound of his father crying one night in June 1959. Slipping out of bed and inching open his bedroom door, he peered out and saw his parents seated on the living-room couch, he testified.

"I heard him say, 'I killed someone,' and then I didn't listen anymore," Norman said.

The young man said he read a magazine article in 1976 about the case, and told his mother about overhearing his father's confession. Shortly after that he was interviewed by RCMP investigators.

Norman's sister, Mrs. Denise Shust, also testified about overhearing her father's confession the same night. Mrs. Shust said she was thirteen when she was awakened by Sandy's voice. She recalled being surprised that he was in the house because her parents were separated at the time.

Listening from behind her bedroom door, she heard Sandy moan: "I have done something terrible." His estranged wife urged him to sit back down and replied that whatever it was he had done, it couldn't have been as bad as he seemed to think it was, Sandy's daughter told the court. Then he began to cry, Mrs. Shust recalled, and blurted out: "We killed a man."

The young woman said she was so shaken and upset when she heard the frightening confession that her mother discovered she had gotten up and ordered her back to bed.

Mrs. Shust also told of her father's visit the day he claimed he had been beaten by his stepdaughter's boyfriend. The witness said her father gave her a letter the next day, instructing her to give it to police if anything bad happened to him.

She learned later that police were looking for the letter, so she read it, then burned it, she said.

"The letter, of what I can remember, said that Katie Harper, former wife of John Down, had smothered John Down and then put him out a window," she testified.

The witness also told the court that in 1974 she and her husband had begun constructing an apartment in the basement of their home for her father to live in because he and Katie were not getting along well. She said she asked him on different occasions during that period if he was responsible for John Down's death, and he always replied that he wasn't.

In later testimony, Sandy and Katie's twenty-year-old daughter, Sherry, added her account of the constant arguments and violence that made the family's home life miserable.

"I don't know him as a father. I know him as someone to be frightened of. He never showed me affection," she said.

"Our mother was our shelter," the witness testified, as her father grimaced and appeared to be fighting back tears. "I can't express what a beautiful woman she is and the love she has."

Breaking into tears when she was accused by Sandy's attorney of not loving her father, she sobbed, "I would love to be able to love my father, to know what it's like to love a father."

RCMP Staff Sergeant Dennis Stewart told the court of Sandy's official statement to police, in which, after years of refusing to cooperate in the investigation, he blamed the murder on Katie.

Sergeant Stewart said that after Sandy was taken to RCMP headquarters in January 1981 in preparation to being formally charged with first degree murder, he at first refused to provide a statement about the death. But as Sandy was washing the ink off his hands after being fingerprinted, Stewart said, he heard him mumble: "I'm not running anymore, I've been running long enough."

Then as Sandy was being transported to the Public Safety Building in Winnipeg, he began to talk to Stewart and to the driver of the car, Sergeant Wayne Lymburner about the murder. Sandy said that too many lies had been told, and that after running for nineteen years, he was too old to run anymore. "I almost drank myself to death. Don't want to see her get off scott free," Sandy was quoted as saying.

It was then, Stewart said, that Sandy denied murdering Down and pointed the finger at Katie as the killer. The Mountie said that Sandy claimed he had taken a bus and hitchhiked to the Down home the night of the murder, and that when he arrived there, the victim "was almost done."

Stewart said that Sandy declared, "I've done a lot of things in my life, but not that. I never killed a man in my life. I couldn't even kill an animal. She done the job herself."

Opening Katie's defense, Attorney Hersh Wolch told the jury that he would produce shocking evidence to show that Sandy was the probable killer of his client's first husband. And he said he would show that Down's killing was an irrational incident, not premeditated homicide as contended by the Crown.

"We know there was foul play; there's no doubt about it," Wolch conceded. "But if you decide it was an irrational act, you may ask which one of the two accused would do an irrational act?" Then he went on to say that he would produce evidence to show that Sandy was a vicious and cruel man, with a lack of sexual control.

The attorney promised to demonstrate that Katie had lived with a double fear throughout her unhappy marriage to Sandy. Not only did she live with a "general fear" of Sandy, Wolch declared, but she was also terrified of being blamed for her first husband's death because she had given him sleeping pills — and an inquest had ruled that Down died of unexplained barbiturate poisoning.

"You will know the sheer hell this woman has gone through," he declared.

When Katie's oldest daughter, Patricia Kathleen Tait, was called to testify in her mother's defense, she confirmed Wolch's promise to produce testimony which would shock the "sensibilities" of the jury. She told the panel that her stepfather had molested her for years as a child and sexually assaulted her on her wedding day.

Speaking in carefully measured tones, the twenty-five-year-old woman said that from the time she was about ten years old Sandy had forced her to bargain sexual favors for clothes and permission to associate with her friends. She said that when she finally mustered the courage to tell her mother about his behavior, Katie was shocked and mortified. "Mom told me I was always to say no and I always said no after that," she testified.

The witness said that when she asked her mother why she stayed with Sandy when she was so obviously unhappy, Katie replied: "I can't leave right now. My life depends on it. I'll tell you later."

Mrs. Tait also told the jury that on her wedding day, her stepfather began choking Katie in the kitchen of their home during the reception. She said that when she tried to intervene, Sandy attacked her sexually.

Testimony by her sister, Daphne Hopkins, shored up the picture of Sandy as a mean-spirited, violent stepfather. She told the jury that when he was drunk he behaved like a wild animal.

"My (step)father horrified us, all of us," she

said. When she attempted to take Katie away to live with her in 1977, Sandy threatened to kill her mother, her daughter testified.

"Don't worry, I'll kill you. You won't get away," she claimed he told Katie. The witness added that she consequently obtained a gun permit and purchased a handgun for protection against her stepfather.

Another witness backed up the story of Sandy's threats against Katie's life. He said he was recruited by the boyfriend of one of Sandy's stepdaughters in 1976 to listen to a quarrel between Sandy and Katie. Admitting that he mistakenly thought he was helping set Sandy up for blackmail or some other scheme, the witness said that he and his companion hid outside the Harper house and listened as Sandy threatened to kill Katie if she blabbed about her first husband's death.

The jury was told that the boyfriend was acting as an informant who arranged for Katie to tell her story to the RCMP, and that she staged the fight, knowing that he would be eavesdropping.

An already convoluted and queer case, the trial took one of its most bizarre twists when Wolch, Katie's attorney proposed giving the jury coffee spiked with sleeping pills, so the jurors could taste for themselves the bitterness of the barbiturate, sodium amytal, which pathologists had found traces of in the victim's body.

This surprising suggestion was immediately objected to by Dangerfield, and Justice Guy Kroft sent the jury from the courtroom. Wolch was anxious to reproduce a taste test conducted by Ruth Diamont, an associate professor at the University of Manitoba on ten men in their twenties. Professor Diamont said that a single capsule of amytal in a cup of coffee was easily detectable by its bitter taste. In fact, she said, it is four times as bitter as caffeine and the taste could not even be masked by milk and sugar.

Although Wolch had brought instant coffee, sugar, milk, a kettle and small serving cups to court, the courtroom experiment was never conducted on the jury. When the panel returned to the courtroom there was no further mention of the test.

The complex six-week trial was nearing an end when the judge permitted the Crown to reopen its case so the jury could hear testimony from a last-minute witness. The witness, identified as a nun, said that during a prison visit more than two years earlier Katie had admitted participating in the murder.

The jury again returned a verdict of guilty of first-degree murder against Katie, and Sandy was convicted of second-degree murder. Katie was sentenced to life in prison with no eligibility for parole for twenty-five years, but was released on bail, pending appeals. Sandy was sentenced to a life term without eligibility for parole for ten years, and was also released on bail pending his appeal. Shortly after the conviction, new controversy was added to the already tangled case when it was learned that the Crown's last minute witness was not, in fact, a nun.

Nine months after the sentencing, the Manitoba Court of Appeals reduced the murder convictions against the couple to manslaughter, and resentenced them to terms of twenty years each. Wolch had argued that the trial judge erred in permitting the Crown to reopen its case near the trial's end in order that the so-called nun could testify.

In arguing Sandy's appeal, Attorney David Margolis contended that his client should be acquitted because none of the evidence at the trial had tied him to the murder, but merely placed him in the house where, by his own admission, he had helped toss the victim's body out a window.

"Throwing a body out a window is not a crime," Justice Joseph O'Sullivan commented. "But it gives rise to an inference that his (Sandy's) presence at the earlier, grisly scene was not innocent."

Katie was transported to the Portage la Prairie Correctional Institute near Winnipeg. Later, despite her and her family's objections, she was transferred to the Ontario women's prison at Kingston, hundreds of miles from her home.

Despite the Appeals Court's ruling reducing the charges and sentences, Wolch disclosed that he would seek yet a third trial for Katie, by asking the Supreme Court of Canada — which had quashed her initial murder conviction — to rule she had been improperly tried. The defense attorney contended that the Attorney General of Manitoba erred in ordering that the Harpers be tried together. Early the next year the court officially refused to hear the new appeal, offering no explanation for its dismissal. Nearly twenty-four years after John Down's death, Canada's longest-running murder case had ended at last.

Four years later, in August 1987, his convicted killers were granted day parole. Sandy was sixty-eight years old; Katie was fifty-four. Conditions of their parole permitted them to work or study in their communities by day, but required they sleep in halfway houses at night. They were scheduled to become eligible for full parole in 1989.

CHAPTER TEN

THE CHAIN-SAWED TORSO

Tom Mosher and his son, Dennis, knew the best fishing holes in that part of the Mississippi River around Davenport that winds under the eastern edge of Iowa and defines the state border with Illinois.

An area just upriver from Davenport, near the city boundary of Bettendorf, Iowa, could sometimes produce a good catch. But it wasn't a fish that had caught the eyes of the anglers on a cool mid-April morning in 1983 when their attention was drawn to a white, bloated object snagged against a large rock near the Iowa shore.

The object turned out to be the gruesome half-torso of a woman, a putrefying chunk of meat that extended from just above the navel to the mid-thighs.

Close inspection of the remains by pathologists with the medical examiner's office in Davenport disclosed an ugly jagged gash more than a foot-and-a-half long on the back of the severed torso. Because edges of the flesh and bones were torn and ragged, the pathologists concluded that a chain saw might have been used in the crude operation. Tissue and blood samples also indicated that the lump of human flesh could have been in the river for a month or more.

It was obvious that whoever had hacked up the body and dumped the parts in the river in an attempt to avoid identification, knew what he or she was doing. In similar cases, after the limbs and head are removed, the torso is usually left whole and body gasses that form during putrefication can cause the remains to float to the surface. Cutting the torso in half eliminated the body gasses, so it was only by chance that the lower portion of the cadaver had been trapped above water by the rock.

With such a small portion of the body to work from, it was difficult for pathologists to immediately learn much about the woman's appearance and physical condition before her death. Although unable to determine her precise age, they estimated she may have been in her thirties.

No one in authority doubted that exact identification of the victim was going to be extremely difficult, unless more of the missing body parts, especially the head, could be recovered. And if they were still in the river, they could be miles upstream from Bettendorf, depending on where they were dumped; or all the way downstream to New Orleans and the Gulf of Mexico.

Police crews in boats were dispatched to the river along and near the passage between Bettendorf and the Rock Island Arsenal on the Illinois side to drag the muddy bottom with grappling hooks. A soggy collection of old tires and other useless junk was snagged and brought to the surface, but no bodies.

Police divers, clad in protective rubber wetsuits, plunged into the chilly river and cruised through the dark water, poking into the mud and silt at every suspicious lump. But their underwater search was as unsuccessful as the effort of the boat crews.

No trace of the upper torso, the arms, legs, or head and neck of the victim was ever found.

However, there still remained other means of finding out who the woman might have been, and officers with the Davenport Police Department's Criminal Investigation Division were determined to solve the grisly puzzle.

Police Corporal Dennis Kern turned to the national crime computer for a list of missing women in Iowa and the neighboring states of Illinois, Wisconsin and Minnesota whose descriptions could fit the general characteristics of the mysterious torso.

Kern came up with a list of seventeen women. Compiled information from the remains indicating that the size of the hips and waist pointed to a woman who could have weighed roughly between 120 and 135 pounds; there were faint stretch marks and other indications that she had been pregnant at least once; her blood type had been discovered; and the color of her pubic hair — which would later become a source of controversy — was described at the autopsy as reddish-brown.

Laboratory comparison of blood samples didn't hold out much promise of linking the remains to any specific woman, although it was useful in eliminating those with non-matching blood types.

Once the list could be narrowed down, another highly sophisticated laboratory technique seemed to offer promise of making a more definite identification. The procedure calls for geneticists and laboratory technicians to examine blood and tissue samples for some seventy enzymes and other substances referred to as genetic markers or genetic fingerprints, inherited from parents.

Consequently, matching the markers lifted from the blood and tissue of the woman with those of the parents of an individual thought to be the victim, could come close to proving positive identification.

After conducting their own tests, Davenport pathologists sent the torso to the Southwestern Institute of Forensic Science in Dallas, Texas, to be examined for genetic markings.

The search for the genetic fingerprints promised to be a long and complicated process, but other developments were shaping up that would provide the break police were looking for in the case.

Investigators were taking a close look at a missing person's report filed with the Davenport Police Department on a local woman who hadn't been seen or heard from by her friends and relatives since about a month before the discovery of the torso in the river.

Mrs. Joyce Klindt was the thirty-three-year-old wife of a prominent Davenport chiropractor, Dr. James Klindt, and the mother of a twelve-year-old son, Bartley. According to a description provided by her husband and entered on the report, she was five feet, four inches tall, weighed 130 pounds, and had brown hair.

The couple had been experiencing serious marital difficulties for some time and Dr. Klindt explained that his wife had walked out on him and their son on March 18. Curiously however, she hadn't confided her plans to her best friends or contacted her parents in Granite City, Illinois. Nor had she apparently given much thought to taking extra clothing along on her flight.

Mrs. Klindt's car was found abandoned in the parking lot of the Holiday Inn, across the Mississippi River Bridge from Davenport in Moline, Illinois. Moline, with Rock Island, Illinois, and Bettendorf and Davenport in Iowa, composes a large metropolitan area of more than 3.5 million people clustered along the two shores of the Mississippi that is known locally as the Quad Cities.

No one at the Moline motel recalled seeing the attractive housewife around the area, and there was no record of her checking in as a guest.

Mrs. Klindt's parents, Eugene and Virginia Monahan, as well as her friends, were puzzled and worried about her strange disappearance. Although she was a notoriously poor housekeeper, they insisted that she was an excellent and devoted mother who kept a close watch on Bart's performance at school and took him virtually everywhere with her. She would hardly have abandoned her son, no matter how serious the rift was in her marriage. And the rift was serious!

Jim Klindt was a handsome, though rapidly balding, six-foot, six-inch tall Davenport native whom fortune had always seemed to smile on. The son of affectionate and generous parents, he was a star track competitor at Davenport West High School where he was one of the most popular boys in his class and had his choice of a host of pretty girls as dates.

But it was vivacious Joyce Monahan, of Granite City, who caught his eye after he set out to follow in his father's footsteps as a chiropractor by beginning studies at the Logan College of Chiropractic in St. Louis, Missouri. Driving a gleaming new Corvette given to him by his parents as a high school graduation present, Jim left Davenport for St. Louis. By the time he graduated from Logan College and returned to Davenport to enter chiropractic practice with his father in shared offices in the spacious family home, Joyce had become Mrs. Klindt, and the young couple had an infant son. Anxious to help them get started, Jim's parents permitted him to use the offices rent free.

It wasn't long before Jim and Joyce, with a $38,000 no-interest loan from his parents, bought their own luxurious home, and were firmly settled into the good life. Jim drove around town in a late model silver Cadillac, and Joyce ran errands, kept appointments with her hairdresser, maintained her many social activities, and delivered her son to and from school and other events, in a shiny Volkswagen Jetta. The couple also owned a third car, a luxury motor home and three boats. Jim even sponsored a ladies bowling team of which Joyce was a member.

Somehow, however, the marriage began to go sour. Joyce's poor housekeeping probably didn't help — it wasn't unusual for her to put off the laundry until the entire family had run out of clean clothes. Nor were Jim and Joyce sharing their lives as they once had. When Jim wasn't working, it seemed he was always out either boating on the river, or taking mysterious drives in the camper.

In September, 1982, Jim met a shapely young hairdresser, Terry Kuehn, at a restaurant in Davenport, and they began dating almost every night. Sometimes they picked up a bottle of wine and made love in his luxury camper. At other times they slipped away to out-of-town restaurants where they weren't likely to be seen by people who knew the prominent chiropractor. During the Christmas holiday that year, while Joyce and Bart were visiting her parents, Terry even spent a night at the Klindt house.

About a week before Christmas, the Klindts went together to an attorney to initiate paperwork for a divorce. The lawyer finally dealt only with the husband, who provided him with financial information and other material he needed to prepare documents for a final decree.

Joyce believed that her husband had changed his mind and the proceedings had been dropped, until she found some divorce documents in his office. She was shocked and angry when she realized that her husband was planning to go through with a "no fault" divorce, and had arranged for settlement terms she considered unacceptable — especially in matters relating to Bart's custody.

One day before a court date that had been set up by her husband for a final decree of divorce, and two days before her disappearance, she showed the documents taken from her husband's office to an attorney she had retained for herself.

The day originally set for the divorce, Joyce confronted her husband in a bitter face off at their home. She told him that not only did she know he was planning to get the divorce, she also knew of the proposed settlement terms — and that he was running around with another woman. She informed him that she had retained her own lawyer who would look out for her interests in any divorce proceedings. The angry encounter quickly developed into a shouting and cursing match.

"I don't like you since you hired this lawyer," Dr. Klindt angrily declared at one point.

After the battle royal finally ended, Joyce knocked at the door of close friends, Donald and Mary Ann Roth and poured out her troubles to Mary Ann. She also gave Mrs. Roth some personal belongings to keep for her, and, unknown to Dr. Klindt, an audio cassette tape of the quarrel she had secretly recorded.

Sympathetic and concerned about her friend, Mary Ann Roth telephoned Joyce the morning after the tape was dropped off and was pleased to find her in much better spirits. Joyce talked of returning to school and said she planned to discuss her situation with the minister of Mrs. Roth's church. After telling her friend that her husband had returned to the house, Joyce hung up the telephone.

That day Joyce vanished from her home.

Sometime after Mrs. Roth had talked with her friend for the last time, Dr. Klindt met his sweetheart for lunch and confided to her that Joyce had left a few hours earlier. Then the couple slipped off to his motor home, which was parked in a shopping center lot, and made love.

When she did not hear again from her friend later in the day, Mrs. Roth became apprehensive, and after making some telephone calls learned that Joyce had missed several appointments. In an effort to locate Joyce, Mrs. Roth telephoned several of her friends and relatives, and made three trips to the Klindt home.

During one of those trips, Dr. Klindt told her that when he came home he found Joyce sitting on the bed with a gun to her head. He said she had left to visit a brother in Pennsylvania for a week after he gave her $2,000.

Mrs. Roth knew Joyce had been talking on the kitchen telephone when her husband came home, and she told Dr. Klindt he was lying.

Joyce's mother, troubled over her daughter's marital difficulties and fearful for her safety, also telephoned the Klindt home that night. She told her son-in-law that her daughter loved him.

"Love," he snapped back, "I don't know what that word means."

To some of the Klindt acquaintances who knew of the couple's domestic troubles, it seemed plausible that she had endured enough of the bickering and misery and abruptly walked out. But to those who knew her better, it was inconceivable that she would go without putting up a spirited fight for her son's custody.

Distressed over their friend's ominous disappearance, the Roths played the tape. They realized that they had evidence that could very likely put Dr. Klindt behind bars. But there wasn't much police could do. Dr. Klindt stuck to his story that his wife had walked out on him. And he told police that after finding her upstairs with a gun — which in this version was purportedly pointed at the floor — he gave her $4,000 (not $2,000 as he told Mrs. Roth) before she left. He didn't show any particular interest in getting her back.

If Joyce had thought things over and returned to the house unexpectedly, she would have been in for a rude surprise. A few days after she disappeared from the house, Dr. Klindt moved his girlfriend in, informing his son and mother that the attractive young woman was his housekeeper.

Then the half torso was fished out of the Mississippi.

Joyce's friends and relatives received news of the grisly discovery with dread, and they set out to gather evidence on their own that she had met with foul play. Police were presented with the tape recording, a diary and some photographs.

The tape was startling. It had barely started to play when a voice identified as the chiropractor's was heard calling his wife dirty names and telling her he hated her. The couple was heard quarreling over how the property should be divided for the divorce, and how to handle custody of their son, Bart.

The most ominous of all the tape's revealed acrimony occurred, however, when the voice identified as Joyce's was heard demanding to know what her husband meant by a threat during an earlier argument to cut her into little pieces. He responded that he was just being dramatic.

The vehement forty-eight minute shouting match finally ended with Klindt storming out of the house.

The attention of investigators was also directed to the diary, which indicated that Dr. Klindt had dabbled with illegal drugs. Photos taken inside his motor home showed marijuana and a suspicious appearing cache of pills.

At last detectives had the evidence they needed to justify a search warrant that would legally get them inside the home. The warrant allowed investigators to search for illicit drugs or evidence of drugs or drug dealing.

They found the drug evidence in the motor home, which was parked in the Klindt driveway. Inside the basement of the house, they found a chain saw, which they seized. Dr. Klindt was arrested on misdemeanor charges of illegal possession of MDA amphetamines, and marijuana. He pleaded guilty to both charges and paid $300 in fines. The chain saw was returned to him, after he filed a petition with the court.

Still, Klindt couldn't be touched with a murder charge, even though investigators managed to reduce the list of missing women whose descriptions seemed to match up with the partial torso, from seventeen names to four — and one of those four was the chiropractor's wife.

Corporal Kern had also done his best to turn up any trace of a living Mrs. Joyce Klindt, checking driver license, car registration and passport records across the country for traces of the missing woman. And he checked additional police reports of unidentified female bodies found in other states, looking for a description that matched that of the Davenport housewife.

Detective Lieutenant Ted Carroll, of the Davenport Police Department's Criminal Investigation Division, who headed the probe, talked to Klindt at police headquarters on different occasions about events leading up to Joyce's disappearance, and each time heard different stories.

The first time Klindt described his activities on the day his wife had vanished, he said that after Joyce left he took his air boat out on the river for a while, then returned home.

The next time Carroll and Klindt talked, he said that after Joyce left he met his girlfriend, then drove his wife's car to the motel in Moline near the Quad-City Airport. Klindt claimed he moved the car because he thought police would try harder to locate his wife if they couldn't find it.

Carroll was puzzled, because the police weren't even looking for Mrs. Klindt at the time her husband said the car was moved.

Joyce had been gone for more than nine months, when authorities in Davenport received a report from the Southwestern Institute of Forensic Science in Dallas: Genetic markers found in the tissues and blood of the half-torso, indicated with 98 percent certainty that the remains were those of the missing Davenport wife and mother. A rare enzyme found in the piece of flesh pulled from the river had been matched with a similar enzyme in the body makeup of one of Joyce's parents.

On March 28, 1984, one year and ten days after Joyce Klindt was reported missing, her husband was arrested for her murder. Lieutenant Carroll, accompanied by uniformed officers, confronted Dr. Klindt at his chiropractic clinic, handed him an arrest warrant and informed him that he was being taken into custody on charges of first-degree murder.

Dr. Klindt's reaction to the lawmen when they walked into his office was a casual "Hi there." Still wearing the blue laboratory coat and brown trousers he had on when he was picked up, and still insisting that his wife was alive somewhere, Dr. Klindt was lodged in the Scott County Jail in Davenport. Bail was set at a staggering one million dollars.

Facing a long term in prison if convicted, the hard-pressed chiropractor sought out the best legal assistance he could find. He settled on Lawrence Scalise, a former Iowa Attorney General from the capital city of Des Moines, and one of the most highly respected criminal defense lawyers in the state.

When Scalise asked the court to trim the unusually high bail for his client, the state disclosed that authorities had information that Dr. Klindt had somehow acquired roadmaps while he was being held in custody. Allegations were also cited by the prosecution indicating that the chiropractor had tried to get witnesses to alter their stories, and that he was a hot-shot drug dealer who had fallen into debt. The bail reduction request was rejected.

The prosecution also geared-up for what promised to be the most sensational murder case ever to originate in Scott County, and one of the most dramatic trials in the state's history. County Attorney William Davis, who had graduated at the top of his class from the Drake University Law School in Des Moines, and who had won convictions in some of the area's most celebrated murder cases, headed the prosecution team.

Davis knew he would face a unique challenge in pressing for a first-degree murder conviction without first having positive identification of the body. There was no head and face, no teeth to be checked against dental records, no fingerprints, and no scars of telltale operations to help prove that the human remains found in the river belonged to Joyce Klindt.

Much of the prosecution's case would depend on the jury's and the court's acceptance of the work accomplished at the forensic laboratories in Dallas and the conclusions of geneticists and pathologists that the half-torso was, indeed, that of the missing homemaker. Yet, the sophisticated technique of tracing genetic markers was still relatively new and untested in the courts.

Scalise and his defense team also had an imposing hurdle to face in convincing a jury that Klindt was innocent of murdering his wife, and that the woman had merely walked out because she was faced with losing her home, husband and child. The tape recording of the quarrel could be damning if the jury believed that Klindt had indeed said he meant to hack his wife into pieces, and was serious about carrying out the threat.

The already bizarre murder case took one more curious twist when Klindt's attorney filed a discovery motion. The motion, which permits the defense to examine documents and other evidence gathered during an investigation, asked among other things, if Scott County Attorney's authorities had been contacted by psychics who knew the whereabouts of the defendant's wife. But if any psychics knew the missing woman was still alive or had tried to locate her, they had failed.

Because of the flash flood of publicity the case attracted in the Quad City area, Scalise petitioned for a change of venue. The trial was subsequently moved 120 miles downriver to Keokuk, a small pastoral town of about 15,000 in Lee County, in the very southeastern tip of the state.

After two days of jury selection, seven men and five women were seated to hear the case against the thirty-six-year-old, big-city chiropractor accused of murdering his wife.

The jury listened for nearly three weeks to the grim story of a disintegrating marriage, vicious quarrels, a philandering husband's backstreet romance — and of the terrible consequences that the prosecution claimed led to the death, dismemberment, and disposal of Joyce Klindt.

"Why did she get killed?" Davis asked about the dead woman. "Because she hired a (divorce) lawyer. She decided to stand and fight. She decided to stand her ground," he insisted.

They heard the defense's contention that the pathetic chunk of meat dragged from the Mississippi River was not Joyce Klindt, and that she was still alive but had dropped out of sight because she was losing her husband and son. "The possibility it is Joyce Klindt is zero," Scalise declared of the partial torso.

Scalise called only one defense witness, Bart Klindt. The boy said he had asked his mother to leave, so that he and his father could find out how they would fare without her after the divorce.

The panel deliberated for twenty-nine hours, over four days, before the foreman reported a deadlock. Reluctantly, Scott County District Judge James R. Havercamp declared a mistrial because of a hung jury.

Iowa criminal law requires that in cases of mistrial, new trials must be rescheduled within ninety days, unless the defendant waives that right or the prosecution is dropped. Judge Havercamp selected Sioux City, a meat-packing center of about 85,000, located some 350 miles west across the state in cattle country along the Missouri River, for the new trial.

Not only was the location changed for the new trial, but certain alterations were also made in the prosecution's tactics. Davis beefed up his expert testimony to better explain the complex information about genetics, blood and tissue testing, and the reading of body marks. He also presented his case in more chronological order than before, and took special pains to group together the witnesses who were testifying about similar subjects so that their testimony would have more impact.

Davis told the jury of ten men and two women that he intended to prove that the half-torso found in the river was that of Joyce Klindt. Then, he said, he would focus on Dr. Klindt's actions and statements during the period of Joyce's disappearance, to prove that the defendant had murdered his wife, sliced up her body with a chain saw, and dumped the pieces in the river.

"You are going to find out he had a motive," the prosecutor declared, which he claimed was Klindt's desire to get rid of his wife so he could live with his girlfriend Terry Kuehn.

Scalise, the lawyer for the defense, charged that the best any expert who studied the body portion could do, was come up with a description so general it would fit millions of women. He derided a statistician's claim that if it was assumed the torso was one of the four missing women from the Midwest, it was about 99 percent probable that it was part of Mrs. Klindt's body. It was the first time, he scoffed, that "anyone has tried to prove a murder by a statistic."

"The torso is not and cannot be a portion of the body of Joyce Klindt," he declared.

Some witnesses who hadn't testified at the first trial were called for the second, while others were dropped. There were also startling surprises in the new testimony.

One of the biggest surprises of the second trial occurred when the defendant's mother, Mrs. Geraldine Klindt, testified that she believed she had seen her daughter-in-law in June or July, some three or four months after Joyce had vanished from her home. Dr. Klindt's mother had not mentioned the incident during the trial in Keokuk.

When the prosecutor questioned Mrs. Klindt about the last time she had seen Joyce, she replied that it was on the evening of Tuesday, March 15, 1983. Then, after pausing, she blurted out: "But I swear to God I saw her drive through the alley in June, or July of 1984."

Outraged, Davis tossed his pen in the air, and demanded to know why she hadn't mentioned the incident during the earlier trial, or said anything to the authorities. She replied that she hadn't been sure of what she had seen until she heard one of her son's friends testify in Keokuk that he thought he had seen Joyce driving a car shortly after her disappearance.

Mrs. Klindt said she was on her back porch when she saw a silver car drive through the alley, and she thought she saw Joyce inside.

"I remember I almost went into shock. I ran into the house and told my husband," she said.

Jan Simmons, who along with his wife, Dixie, were close friends of the Klindts, had sprung a surprise on the prosecution during the first trial when he testified that he saw a woman he thought to be Joyce driving a silver-colored car in Davenport some time after she had last been seen at her home in March, 1983. He repeated essentially the same story during the second trial in Sioux City.

Simmons said he was driving west when he glanced at the car next to him and saw a woman he thought was Joyce. He said the woman turned her head away, and then drove onto another street. He followed but couldn't catch up with her again, Simmons testified. The witness said he couldn't get the license plate number, but thought the plate was yellow with white numbers. A policeman later testified that he had checked all the states and provinces of Canada and couldn't find a license plate with those color combinations.

Even though she and her husband were called as prosecution witnesses, Dixie Simmons had also provided testimony favorable to the defense at the first trial. She said she had seen Joyce nude at different times, and after viewing photographs of the torso, didn't think it was part of her friend's body.

Several riverside residents and restaurant employees provided testimony that placed Dr. Klindt on the Mississippi in his airboat on the chilly, rainswept day his wife had dropped out of sight. A restaurant employee said she watched a man put a garbage bag onto an airboat, take it out into the river, return without it, and repeat the process about five times. "Who's that crazy ass out on the river?" she said she had commented.

She was the only witness to testify about seeing the man placing the bags on the airboat. But others identified the man seen with the water craft as Klindt. As the Mississippi was exceptionally high that day, several witnesses said Klindt's boat was the only one they saw on the river.

But just as in the Keokuk trial, the hardest-fought element of the trial focused on the prosecution's efforts to prove that the torso belonged to the missing Davenport homemaker.

The opposing attorneys contested the size of Joyce's hips, arguing as to whether they were relatively slender, or broad enough to fit the half-torso; whether or not moles and birthmarks on the remains could be matched with the missing woman's body was also argued as well as the actual color of her hair.

Pinpointing the color of the pubic hair found on the partial corpse to see if it matched with Joyce's, required several witnesses, and elicited a variety of answers.

Hairdresser Patti Hummel did not testify at the first trial, but when she was called to the stand in Sioux City, she said Joyce's natural hair color was light brown with a slight reddish tint. Mrs. Hummel, who had styled Joyce's hair from 1971 to 1976, was shown a sample of pubic hair taken from the half-torso, and agreed that the color matched Joyce's. Her description of the missing woman's hair coloring also matched that of the doctor who had performed the autopsy.

The hairdresser said that the frosting she had applied to Joyce's hair could have made it appear a dishwater blonde, and, in Keokuk, Mrs. Monahan had testified that her daughter's hair was a dishwater blonde color. However, at the trial in Sioux City, she said the color of Joyce's hair was hard to pin down, but had a red tint to it with some brown and some blonde coloring, and that both her sons were redheads.

A world reknowned forensic anthropologist, a statistician, a geneticist, a dermatologist and two experts on blood and tissue, were called by the prosecution to support the contention that the body part was Joyce Klindt's.

It was testified that Joyce had type A blood, the same blood type found in the torso. A blood and tissue expert from the Dallas laboratories said that, based on her studies of genetic factors, she had concluded that the torso could not only be from the daughter of Mrs. Klindt's parents, but from the mother of Bart Klindt as well. She said it was 107.8 times more likely that Mr. and Mrs. Monahan would produce the types of enzymes or genetic factors that were found in the tissues of the torso, than if a couple were selected at random.

After pointing out in cross-examination that millions of couples could produce a child with the same genetic markers as those found in the torso, Scalise asked the witness if she was saying that the chances of the torso being or not being Joyce Klindt were equal.

"No, it's more likely that it is than it is not," she replied, "but not by a very high level."

A statistician from the University of Iowa, said it was a 99 percent probability that the torso belonged to Joyce. An important part of his conclusion was based on the list of missing women in the Midwest provided to him by police who worked from the national crime computer. And that created one of the trial's new surprises.

Corporal Kern testified that since the earlier trial he had learned that five Chicago women reported as missing during the period of time before the partial torso was found, had not been entered on the national crime computer when he compiled his list.

As important as recitation of dry statistics and sophisticated discussion of genetics were to the trial, the high point for most courtroom observers occurred with the appearance of Dr. Klindt's pretty paramour, Terry Kuehn, who testified as the final prosecution witness.

The slender young hairdresser was wearing a tan skirt and matching jacket over a turquoise sweater when she took the stand in Sioux City. Speaking softly, she told about meeting Dr. Klindt in September, 1982, and of the love affair that ensued. She told of trips with him to Las Vegas, the Bahamas, the Wisconsin Dells — a resort area of picturesque wooded canyons and river rapids — and to other locations. Her lover's son went along on some of the trips, she said, but stayed in separate rooms.

Before Joyce disappeared, she and Klindt told the boy that she was a maid, the witness said.

The day of the disappearance, she met Klindt for lunch and he told her that his wife had left that morning. Later that day they went to his motor home and made love. She said she saw her lover the next day and they had sex again.

In September, 1983, approximately six months after Joyce's disappearance, she moved into the Klindt house, Miss Kuehn informed the Court.

She and her lover also became much more open about their relationship after Joyce dropped out of sight, dining together in Davenport restaurants, and boating together on the river.

Once again, the Klindt's son Bart was the only defense witness, and the last to testify. He repeated his testimony that he had suggested to his mother that she leave her home so that he and his father could see how well they got along without her.

In his closing arguments, Davis told the jury that Joyce was killed because she finally decided to stand up to her husband, and insisted that it was a portion of her body that had been pulled from the Mississippi.

He said that "all hell broke loose" when she hired an attorney after discovering that her husband was going through with the divorce she had thought he called off. "Jim Klindt was upset. No one had told him 'no' before," the prosecutor declared.

Davis suggested that Klindt strangled his wife with his powerful hands, (strengthened in his chiropractic practice) before cutting her up with a chain saw and dumping the pieces in the river.

Attorney John Sandre, who joined Scalise on the defense team for the second trial, charged in his summation that the prosecution had presented a case based on an attack of Klindt's upbringing and lifestyle. Sandre conceded that Klindt's philandering and some of the other things the jury had heard about the defendant indicated he had imperfections in his character. "But it is not the stuff that murders are made of," he declared.

Scalise also cautioned the jury not to be swayed by moral judgments based on testimony about Klindt's extramarital fling.

"The purpose of that," he said, "is to make you so angry that you jump to the conclusion that an adulterer is also a murderer."

Continuing to focus on the contention that Joyce was not murdered by her husband, but fled from her home, he said that when her son, Bart, suggested she leave it was the most fundamental rejection.

"Given what you know, I think you have to conclude that that's sufficient reason to leave," he said.

The jury deliberated for fifteen hours over a two-day period before returning a verdict of guilty to second-degree murder. As the verdict was read, Klindt slumped and permitted his head to drop between his knees, but quickly recovered and sat up straight again.

The jury decision was believed to mark the first time in modern Iowa history that a murder conviction was won by the prosecution without positive identification of a body, and one of only a few such cases in the entire country.

Second-degree murder in Iowa carries a mandatory fifty-year prison term. First-degree murder, which in Iowa indicates premeditation, carries a life sentence in prison without parole.

Back in Davenport, about three weeks after the verdict was returned, Judge Havercamp sentenced Dr. Klindt to a term of up to fifty years in prison. He would become eligible for parole in ten years. Dr. Klindt is serving his sentence at the Iowa Men's Reformatory at Animosa.

* * * * *

Serial Thrill Killers*

They are nightmares become reality—savage, remorseless assassins who butcher for the sheer pleasure of killing. Self-appointed death angels, they select their victims from among the weak, unprotected, unwary, and convenient.

They are serial killers.

Some experts use terms like "recreational homicide" when describing the crazed acts of the men and women who kill once, then again and again. For them, taking a life—sometimes after submitting a victim to terrible torture, rape, and other perversions—can be a means of relieving tension or simply a way to fill in the long hours on an otherwise boring evening. It can be a completely casual, random act perpetrated on a victim selected by the merest chance or accident. Stabbing and strangling are favorite means of murder for serial killers. It's more personal than guns.

Victims are likely to be prostitutes, topless dancers, hitchhikers, transients, runaways, the very young or the very old. Serial killers look for the helpless. One highly respected crime consultant describes them as the most cowardly of criminals. They are excited by power, domination, the ability to control, and the opportunity to play God by choosing who will live and who will die.

Psychologists say serial killers are more difficult to explain than mass murderers, who suddenly slaughter

*© 1990 BY CLIFFORD L. LINEDECKER

a number of people in a single orgy of violence. Mass murderers are often set off by a personal trauma such as loss of a job, a missed promotion, a divorce or other romantic rejection. The victims may be people close to them or total strangers.

Unlike the case with most murders, the victims of serial killers are almost always strangers. And their murders are carefully crafted, carried out—and covered up.

Most of the 20,613 homicides committed in the United States during 1986 (the last year for which figures were available at this writing) involved relatives, friends, associates from work, or other acquaintances. But a disproportionate number of the approximately 30 percent of those homicides that were still unsolved a year later are believed by law enforcement authorities to be serial murders.

Ted Bundy, who admitted only hours before his execution in Florida's "Old Sparky" early in 1989 that he murdered twenty-three young women (he never confessed to the three Florida slayings he was convicted of), and is believed to have taken the lives of many more in a terrible bicoastal spree of kidnap, rape and murder, is the archetypal serial killer.

He was not only intelligent, smooth, and charming, but he always selected victims from among young women whom he had never met before. Murderers who have had no previous contact with their victims until their single fatal encounter can be extremely difficult for law enforcement authorities to track down.

As recently as 1966 only 6 percent of U.S. homicides investigated by police produced no known motive. By the early 1980s, unknown-motive homicides had soared to more than 20 percent. The percentages are still climbing.

There are more than thirty-five thousand known murderers in U.S. prisons, including approximately fifteen hundred on death row. But criminologists believe that many more than that are prowling the streets because they were never caught or never convicted of their crimes. And some experts are estimating, as well, that the perpetrators of more than 40 percent of the murders committed in the United States today are escaping justice. A staggering number of the elusive criminals are serial killers.

Who are they, and why do they kill?

In the past decade, these questions have provoked increasing concern on the part of criminologists and law-enforcement authorities. National, state, and local studies have been funded and staffed with some of the most knowledgeable and respected experts available from universities and police agencies.

They have come up with a plethora of conclusions, recommendations, suppositions, and theories. Serial killers, they tell us, suffered head injuries during childhood. They were bastards, came from broken homes or from one-parent families. They were beaten by alcoholic parents, their mothers were prostitutes or overbearing, and their fathers were weak or unaffectionate. They were sexually abused as children, or exposed to violent pornography, or were victimized by drugs.

It's true that some of those factors exist in the background of some serial killers. Bundy's mother spent her pregnancy in a home for unwed mothers, and shortly before his execution he blamed pornography for inspiring his violence. Velma Barfield (whose outrageous crimes are chronicled in chapter 8) was a prescription medicine junkie and claimed that when she was a teenager she was raped by her father. Carroll Eugene Cole (chapter 5) blamed his bloody rampage against female barflies on traumatic experiences in his home life during his childhood and adolescence.

Millions of other people who never kidnapped,

raped, or murdered, however, can point to similar unfortunate incidents and circumstances in their lives. The sad truth is, no one has yet come up with a valid explanation for why one person becomes a serial killer and another, with similar life experiences or background, does not.

But they know that sex and power are prime motives.

Although many criminologists believe that most serial killers are primarily sadistic sexual psychopaths, in the broad sense of the term they are not insane. They know exactly what they are doing. They're clever, and they tend to plan their crimes and their coverups carefully.

An FBI study of thirty-six convicted serial killers found that most were either psychopathic or sociopathic personalities who felt sexually inadequate or had previous unhappy experiences with women. There are others with different personalities and different motives, of course. There are killers like Michael and Susan Carson, Donald "Peewee" Gaskins, Rudy Bladel, and Velma Barfield—all chronicled in this book. None of them fit the description of sexual psychopath, but their motives were as darkly sinister and they were every bit as deadly as more widely known, sexually motivated butchers like sadistic homosexual John Wayne Gacy, Jr., Boston Strangler Albert DeSalvo, and Bundy.

Whatever their motives, they are a special breed of killer, and their number, as well as the dark roster of their victims, is rapidly increasing.

Today, law-enforcement officers track them with computers, specially trained experts lecture at police seminars focusing on the crimes, and extraordinary efforts are made to coordinate investigations by police agencies from a bewildering variety of jurisdictions.

The U.S. Justice Department's Regional Information Sharing System sponsors seven Regional Crime and Information Centers around the nation to gather data on violent crimes and organize conferences for police officers.

The FBI operates the Violent Criminal Apprehension Program (VI-CAP), a computer-assisted system which correlates crime information from records of homicides reported by many of the nation's seventeen thousand police agencies. It also assists investigators by making available the services of a special Behavioral Science Unit at the Bureau's academy on the Marine base at Quantico, Virginia. The unit helps develop psychological profiles of serial killers and provides other information.

VI-CAP was instrumental in linking a Tampa, Florida man arrested on an apparently unrelated rape charge in 1984 to a particularly grisly crime spree that had baffled police for mouths: a series of murders of prostitutes, topless dancers, and other young women in the Tampa area. Bobby Joe Long was ultimately given two death sentences, pleaded guilty to seven other slayings, and while in prison admitted to a tenth.

Incredible as it may seem, however, even when serial killers are caught and convicted, they are often paroled. In Canada, they are sometimes granted day-long leaves from maximum security prisons and allowed to roam old haunts where they previously terrorized, raped, and murdered.

Savage killers like John Gacy and Wayne Clifford Boden (chapter 10) become model prisoners. Beating the system can be an entertaining and exciting part of the game for serial slayers.

Bundy took great pleasure in obstructing the system. The smirking multiple sex slayer escaped from a Colorado jail, staged an outrageous comic-strip courtroom marriage, boasted that he fathered a child in a prison visiting room, won three stays of execution, ran up a taxpayer bill of six million dollars for legal expenses, and made a string of judges and attorneys look like pitiful circus clowns during an exhausting decade-long encampment on Florida's death row.

When he was at last executed for the murder of a twelve-year-old girl he raped, tortured, and dumped in a pigsty, the public was so fed up by the legal hijinks that they congregated outside the prison by the hundreds to dance, chant, and burn sparklers in celebration of his death. Private citizens were sending a blunt message that the men and women in the ponderously muddled justice system didn't seem to grasp. Dealing with serial killers isn't a silly game for a few venal lawyers and misguided do-gooders to play out in the nation's courtrooms. Punishment should fit the crime!

Capital punishment does indeed prevent serial killers from ever killing again. No one has ever provided any valid evidence that serial killers can be rehabilitated. But murderers who are executed can never escape or be paroled to hunt down and slaughter new victims.

A society that refuses to execute its most monstrous killers is making a dangerous statement: that it will not protect its own citizens and that there is nothing so sacred than it is worth defending at the price of life.

Some behavior is simply so vile and disgusting that the interests of justice cry out for and demand the ultimate penalty.

We hope you have enjoyed this
KNIGHTSBRIDGE book.

We love good books just as you do,
so you can be assured that the
KNIGHT ON THE HORSE
stands for good reading, every time.